A SENSE OF PLACE

A SENSE OF PLACE

*The Best of
British Outdoor Writing*

EDITED BY ROLY SMITH

MICHAEL JOSEPH
LONDON

MICHAEL JOSEPH LTD

Published by the Penguin Group
27 Wrights Lane, London W8 5TZ
Penguin Putnam Inc., 375 Hudson Street, New York, New York 10014, USA
Penguin Books Australia Ltd, Ringwood, Victoria, Australia
Penguin Books Canada Ltd, 10 Alcorn Avenue, Toronto, Ontario, Canada M4V 3B2
Penguin Books (NZ) Ltd, 182–190 Wairau Road, Auckland 10, New Zealand

Penguin Books Ltd, Registered Offices: Harmondsworth, Middlesex, England

First published 1998
1 3 5 7 9 10 8 6 4 2

Set in 11/14½ pt Monotype Plantin Light
Typeset by Rowland Phototypesetting Ltd, Bury St Edmunds, Suffolk
Printed in England by Clays Ltd, St Ives plc

A CIP catalogue record for this book is available from the British Library

ISBN 0 7181 4206 3

The moral right of the editor has been asserted

CONTENTS

Britain's best-known mountaineer is Sir Chris Bonington, a man who has proved, through his presidency of the British Mountaineering Council and the Council for National Parks, a great diplomat and ambassador for the outdoors. Renowned for expeditions to remote peaks in the farthest corners of the globe, Chris gets just as much satisfaction from exploring the riggs and combes of his Cumbrian homeland.

John Cleare, the doyen of British mountain photographers, owns the Mountain Camera Picture Library. He is a veteran of many expeditions to the high mountains of the world. But, surprisingly, he came close to death in usually benign Wessex, where he now lives, and where the sense of the timeless past (and perhaps an extraterrestrial future?) pervades every scene.

Paddy Dillon
Undiscovered Ireland   18

Despite the evidence of his name and his overriding passion for all things Irish, Paddy Dillon is a Lancastrian born and bred. But ever since he first discovered the delights of the Emerald Isle, Paddy has been the greatest advocate for walking in Ireland, even when most editors of outdoor publications overly concerned at 'the Troubles' showed little interest.

Richard Gilbert
The Great Wilderness   31

The accomplished mountaineer and award-winning writer Richard Gilbert has been visiting the North West Highlands for nearly fifty years. For this retired York schoolmaster, the area's unique combination of sea and mountain wilderness is quite simply the most exquisitely beautiful corner of Britain, and the last great wilderness in these islands.

Peter Gillman
In the Footsteps of the Giants   46

Award-winning journalist and author Peter Gillman, a former Sunday Times *staffer and regular contributor to many national newspapers, had the finest apprenticeship anyone could wish for in climbing in the Scottish hills in winter. Then he was bitten by the Munro bug and returned to rediscover the Scottish winter, first leading, then being led by, his son as he strove to complete this perverse mountain marathon.*

Mike Harding
The Striding Dales 61

Writer, photographer and entertainer Mike Harding's lifelong love affair with the Yorkshire Dales began when he was a lad of fourteen and he cycled from his Manchester home to Ribblesdale to climb the 'crouching lion' of Pen-y-Ghent. Today, when not on tour or exploring in the Himalaya, Mike lives in Dent, close to what he describes as 'one of the great walks in the world'.

Terry Marsh
Beyond the Seas of Sorrow 68

Thirty years of visiting the enchanted Island of Skye has only served to further whet Guild secretary Terry Marsh's appetite and longing for the magical 'winged isle'. This former local government officer is now a successful freelance author, editor and journalist, living near Preston in his home county of Lancashire.

Rennie McOwan
A Kind of Paradise 81

The respected Stirling-based journalist, author and broadcaster Rennie McOwan is the alter ego *of Percy Unna, champion and benefactor of Scottish wild country. Rennie is an expert on the history of access to the Scottish hills, and a vociferous campaigner for walkers' rights north of the Border. But his heart is in his local hills, the Ochils, those smooth-sided precursors of the greater mountains further north.*

Jim Perrin
Befriending the Raven 98

Jim Perrin is arguably the finest and most accomplished of contemporary British writers on the outdoors. His work is always elegant, literate and unfailingly passionate on subjects where he feels things are going wrong, because, above all, Jim Perrin cares. *And he cares most intensely about his home country of Wales, whose Welshness is personified for him by his 'dark and cosmic friend', the raven.*

Kev Reynolds
Greensand Roots 111

Kev Reynolds, originally an Essex man and youth hostel warden, now Alpine walking specialist and one of our most respected outdoor writers, lives close to the lush, well-wooded Greensand Ridge between the North and South Downs. This subtle, secret landscape is only twenty-five miles from the heart of London, but it has become the place where this particular nomad could put down his roots.

Richard Sale
The Spirit of Dartmoor 124

Dick Sale is perhaps best known in the outdoor world as an Arctic expert, spending at least a part of every year beyond the 66th parallel. But this writer and research scientist with a doctorate in theoretical physics is never happier than when exploring his home ground of Dartmoor, often dubbed the last wilderness in southern Britain.

Doug Scott
This Other Eden 137

Doug Scott, champion of the Alpine-style ascent of the highest Himalayan peaks, had lived on the edge of the Lake District for five years before he discovered his own special place was right on his doorstep. A mere half-hour bike ride away from his Cumbrian home were the sandstone crags of Armathwaite, a paradise appropriately found by the banks of the River Eden.

Roger Smith
A Singular Place   146

Roger Smith, former editor of The Great Outdoors *and* Environment Now *and from 1994 to 1998 Walking Development Officer for the Scottish Borders, is a Cairngorms devotee. His love of these high and lonely summits has been built up over thirty years of walking and climbing among their high lochans, sparkling burns and cliff-fringed corries. He believes these windswept semi-Arctic summits are a singular, but threatened, place.*

Roly Smith
The Kinder Caper   158

Kinder Scout, the mucky monarch of the Peak, has a special place in the affections of most northern ramblers. After many years of working towards its protection as Head of Information Services with the Peak District National Park, OWG chairman and award-winning author and journalist Roly Smith, now editor of Peak & Pennine *magazine, is no exception.*

Christopher Somerville
A Whisper in the Wind   172

Daily Telegraph *walking correspondent and prolific author Christopher Somerville admits to having a taste for unfashionable countryside. He divides his time between his native Mendip Hills and his house in the centre of Bristol, but loves to seek out the 'shifting mirage' that is East Anglia.*

Walt Unsworth
The Land of Lost Content   186

OWG president Walt Unsworth, a former Mancunian now living on the edge of the Lake District at Milnthorpe, is well known as the co-founder of Cicerone Press, which produces walkers' and climbers' guides. For this award-winning writer and experienced world traveller, the Shropshire hills might seem a strange choice for his favourite place, but when Walt was a teacher in Wolverhampton, they were his 'happy highway'.

Stephen Venables stunned the world of mountaineering when he climbed the 'unclimbable' Kangshung Face of Everest in 1988. But like so many of our contributors, his favourite climbing haunt is much closer to home. The Avon Gorge on the edge of Bristol is Stephen's special place – and 'a glorious gift' to the crag rat.

For John Wyatt, chief ranger of the Lake District National Park for twenty-six years, the chance to actually live and work in the place of his dreams was a passport to heaven. He recorded his escape back to nature in his memorable first book, The Shining Levels. *And even now, after a lifetime's acquaintance, this former Manchester newspaper copyboy finds it impossible to pick a favourite place, walk or fell.*

THE ILLUSTRATORS

David Bellamy
(dust jacket water-colour)

Award-winning water-colourist David Bellamy's love for the great out-doors is matched only by his passionate concern for the environment. Many of his paintings show the honest effects of being executed in the open air – which is David's preferred studio. He spent his childhood in South Wales, where he now lives and works as a full-time artist, author and highly regarded teacher of this most difficult of mediums.

Brian Evans
(frontispiece and chapter-head drawings)

Brian Evans is a director of Carnmor Print and Design, and production director of Cicerone Press. Trained at Leeds Art College, he started drawing for outdoor magazines such as Climber *in the 1960s, and his sensitive pen-and-wash sketches have since illustrated many books. These include his own award-winning guidebooks, many of which are produced in partnership with his wife, Aileen.*

THE OUTDOOR WRITERS' GUILD
The Voice of Outdoor Journalism

The Outdoor Writers' Guild is the only group of media professionals in the UK whose members are exclusively involved in the outdoor world. Increasingly, as its reputation and influence has grown, it has become known as 'the Voice of Outdoor Journalism'.

The Guild was formed in 1980 by a group of journalist friends attending the annual Camping and Outdoor Leisure Association (COLA) Show at Harrogate. From these small and mainly social beginnings, the Guild has expanded rapidly in recent years both in its professionalism and membership. It now has over two hundred members, whose interests cover an impressive range of communication skills. These range from advertising, design and illustration, through audio-visual work, lecturing, broadcasting and film production, photography and guiding, as well as publishing and writing. Membership of the OWG is open to any media professional who is actively involved in informal recreation in the countryside. Qualification is strictly vetted by the Guild Committee, and the membership continues to grow as new skills are included. Most of the best-known media professionals currently working in the outdoor world are members of the Guild, and many have contributed to this anthology.

The aim of the OWG is to promote, encourage and assist the development and maintenance of professional standards among those involved in all aspects of outdoor journalism.

This is achieved through the provision of guidelines and codes of practice for members, and the organization of seminars, workshops and conferences.

The Guild supports the activities of its members by the provision of up-to-date information about factual and technical matters through its journal *Bootprint*. It also represents its members' interests and provides advice to them, acting on their behalf collectively and individually where appropriate. A forum is provided for members through facility trips, meetings and through social events.

Among the other activities undertaken by the Guild is the publication of an annual *Handbook and Directory*, which lists all members and their professional activities and specialisms.

In pursuit of its aim of raising standards, the Guild gives annual awards for excellence achieved by its members. The most important of these are the OWG/COLA Awards for Excellence – an independently judged competition for members who have published books, articles or photographs during the past year. The Guild also presents the *Golden Boot* to the person or company exhibiting at the COLA show who has made an outstanding contribution to the outdoor trade.

The prestigious OWG *Golden Eagle* Award – in the form of an original painting – is presented at the Guild's annual dinner to the person, a member of the Guild or not, who has rendered distinguished or meritorious service to the outdoor world in general. A separate Award for Photographic Excellence is presented at the same occasion.

A Sense of Place

Roly Smith

CHAIRMAN, OUTDOOR WRITERS' GUILD

Consult the genius of the place in all:
That tells the waters to rise and fall;
Or helps th' ambitious hill the heavens to scale,
Or scoops in circling theatres the vale;
Calls in the country, catches opening glades,
Joins willing woods, and varies shades from shades . . .

ALEXANDER POPE (1688–1744)

The eighteenth-century poet Pope was the first to apply Virgil's idea of *genius loci,* or the spirit of the place, to an appreciation of the British landscape. It was an attempt to explain the inexplicable – that subconscious, almost subliminal feeling that a well-loved landscape can impart on the mind of the person held in its thrall.

We all have those special places – the places we go when we want to clear our heads of everyday worries, a crisis at the office or, in the case of the writer, an impending and seemingly impossible deadline. To most of the writers I know, and certainly all of the contributors to this book, these are vital escape routes, where the walk or climb not only exercises the limbs but also recharges the batteries, sorts out the mental processes and generally puts things back into their proper perspective.

This is recreation in its true and original sense, before the word became devalued by the countryside managers to its present debased meaning of mere physical exercise. Recreation really means to re-create, refresh, and reinvigorate.

The writers whose work appears in this anthology are not by any means the first to discover this phenomenon. All the great nature writers, from Thoreau to Whitman, and from Clare to Manley Hopkins, knew it to be an inescapable truth, and that the source of their inspiration lay in the countryside. Even best-selling authors, like Charles Dickens and Hilaire Belloc, realized the thought-clearing benefit of a walk, and the historian George Macaulay Trevelyan encapsulated it in the opening lines of his famous 1913 essay on 'Walking':

> *I have two doctors, my left leg and my right. When body and mind are out of gear (and those twin parts of me live at such close quarters that the one always catches melancholy from the other) I know that I have only to call in my doctors and I shall be well again.*

The favourite operating theatre for Trevelyan's two doctors was Northumberland, from where he thought he could see both heaven and earth, and where he knew he could walk all day on the long ridges of his beloved 'land of far horizons'.

For Romantics like William Wordsworth and Samuel Taylor Coleridge, the same kind of inspiration was provided by the English Lake District. Wordsworth's opium-influenced friend Thomas De Quincey once wrote, perhaps a trifle enviously, that to Wordsworth walking was 'a mode of exertion which, to him, stood in the stead of alcohol and all other stimulants whatsoever to the animal spirits; to which, indeed, he was indebted for a life of unclouded happiness, and we for much of what is most excellent in his writings'.

If walking and climbing in the Great Outdoors is a drug,

then all the authors in this book will happily admit that they are incurable addicts. They were each asked to provide an essay on their favourite place, climb or walk in Britain and explain why it was so special. I suspect many will have kept their really special places to themselves – I know I have. It's the old dilemma for a sensitive outdoor writer: if you write about that special place in glowing terms, the next time you go, you probably won't have it to yourself any more and it might be irreversibly changed by your own thoughtlessness.

If there is one common denominator in this richly diverse collection of writing by the best of British outdoor journalists, it is that indefinable sense of place – Virgil and Pope's *genius loci* – which is so important to the writers. You'll find it in Kev Reynolds's evocative study of his Greensand Ridge Kentish homeland, but equally in mountain-man John Cleare's surprising but affectionate regard for the gentle downs and hill-forts of Wessex. For Dick Sale, an expert on the high Arctic, the moody moorscapes of Dartmoor are where he feels at home, while Housman's 'Land of Lost Content' calls world-traveller Walt Unsworth back to the gentle Shropshire Hills of his youth. The broad skies and windswept marshes of East Anglia are Christopher Somerville's favourite bit of wild country.

Many contributors who made their names in mountaineering with epic struggles up some of the world's highest and most difficult peaks relate gripping, near-death experiences on the relatively humble hills and cliffs of home, like John Cleare and Stephen Venables. In company with the latter, Chris Bonington and Doug Scott, the two other Everest summiteers featured in the book, find that the drama, challenge and beauty of their backdoor hills and crags can match anything they've seen elsewhere in the world. Scotland is the wildest part of Britain so, not unexpectedly, it figures strongly in this anthology. The great wilderness of the North West Highlands is where Richard

Gilbert would usually most like to be, while the semi-Arctic majesty of the Cairngorms attracts Roger Smith and Peter Gillman, especially when it resumes its geologically recent Ice Age persona in the depths of winter. For Guild secretary Terry Marsh, nothing can beat the magical isle of Skye, while Rennie McOwan prefers the voluptuously rolling and grass-clad Ochils, within walking distance of his home in Stirling.

Lancastrian John Wyatt realized his fondest dreams when he came to work in the Lake District for twenty-six years as chief ranger for the National Park, while Mancunian Mike Harding chose Dentdale in the northern part of the Yorkshire Dales as his secure base, far from the glitter and glare of his successful career in show-business.

Paddy Dillon, despite his name and inclination, is another Lancastrian but surely by now an honorary Celt. His heart lies across the stormy Irish Sea in the beautiful knocks and loughs of Northern Ireland. Another writer who has found his roots in a Celtic kingdom is Jim Perrin, whose life-long love affair with Wales shines through in his award-winning prose.

It has been a great pleasure for me to collect and read these essays, which I know have been a labour of love for most of the contributors. Illustrators David Bellamy and Brian Evans have also, as always, put much of their own personal feelings for the outdoors into their sympathetic and equally evocative painting and drawings.

I do hope you enjoy this collection of the best of British outdoor journalism, exclusively by members of the Outdoor Writers' Guild, as much as I did putting it together. Another quote from Alexander Pope seems best to sum up the result:

True wit is nature to advantage dressed,
What oft was thought, but ne'er so well expressed.

THE MOST BEAUTIFUL PLACE
IN THE WORLD
Chris Bonington

I believe the Lake District is as beautiful as anywhere in the
world – the shapes of hill and dale, the lakes themselves, the
subtlety of colour and the harmony of man's impact on this
environment with the patterns formed by dry-stone walls and
the cottages and farmhouses. The one problem is the number
of people, which grows every year, attracted by that beauty.
Yet even on a Bank Holiday it is possible to escape the crowds
by exploring the hills on the edge of the Lakes. I have always
loved Swindale in the eastern fells for its gentle quietness, and
Gouther Crag is another of my favourites. Prow-like buttresses
nestle among gnarled old trees above the level valley bottom,

I

CHRIS BONINGTON

and it has a rural, rather than mountainous, feel, yet the walk Wendy and I took to the top of Selside Pike (2142 ft/653 m) had an amazing variety of views and terrain.

Narrow lanes lead up from Bampton on to the open moor at the bottom of Swindale, where a dreary pumping station and railed roads built by the water company conceal the hidden delights ahead. The valley narrows, with the tree-clad bluff of Bewberrow Crag acting as a gatehouse. A cattle grid and slate notice, stating that there is no parking beyond this point, makes this an obvious start for our walk.

A grassy bridleway crosses the slope above the road, giving access to the brow of the low-flung ridge line just above. Then it is easy walking over well-cropped grass below the crest of the broad, rolling ridge that leads up to Selside Pike. A short way along, a fence cuts across at right angles, but there is a gate close to the edge of the steep drop into Swindale where the wall comes up from the valley. We glimpsed Gouther Crag over the tops of the trees, a red-clad climber just visible on the crest of one of its buttresses.

A shepherd on his four-wheel-drive buggy went past us, his dog ranging widely to gather in the scattering of sheep. Grey, broken clouds with the occasional patch of blue allowed shafts of sunlight to dapple the fells. A hare broke away from just in front of us but our dog Bella, who would have chased after it only a few years ago, barely noticed it. We followed winding sheep tracks that wandered and vanished but took us in the right direction.

The head of the valley now opened out in a steep cirque surrounding the walled fields of the valley bottom, a farmhouse with a jumble of barns clinging to the edge. A steep little gully with part-hidden waterfalls cut through the cirque with a dark gash, while to the left Mosedale Beck tumbled down a gorge.

2

We were about to cross the footpath between the head of Swindale and Haweswater, lightly trodden by central Lakes standards but even so a couple of groups of walkers were already on this veritable main road. We were glad to be crossing it, to regain our solitude, as we picked our way up the broad ridge leading towards the top of Selside Pike. A few false summits and we were upon its rounded dome of grass-covered peat. A tight half-circle of stones sheltered us from a biting wind as we ate our lunch. A skylark soared above, marking out its territory.

It's a fine viewpoint, looking over the Eden Valley and Shap to the east, the limeworks near the head of Shap an eyesore that spent the entire day in a little pool of sunlight while the clouds threw shadows all around it and over the fells. The shapely Howgills contain the south-eastern horizon.

From the summit, you can see most of Haweswater with the deeply hollowed-out bowl of Blea Water, whose containing walls form such a superb cascade of ice in winter, its eastern retaining ridge making a dramatic sweep straight to the top of High Street, site of the Roman road leading over the eastern fells. Looking south-west the view is restricted by the broad summits of other tops to the ridge while to the south the fells form a swell of moorland more reminiscent of the Peak District than the Lakes.

We decided to cut down into the valley of Mosedale, to return easily to Swindale, but if we had had more energy we could have continued over two tops to Artlecrag Pike, which would have given wider views to the west and south into Longsleddale. A fence forms a right angle on the top of Selside Pike, but you can crawl under it without doing damage. We followed it down to the col, where we broke away left to contour round the shoulder of Howes to drop down into Mosedale.

It's a wide sweeping valley that feeds off the beaten track. The spoil of an old quarry scars the flank of the hill while below it is an old cottage that still has its roof.

A group of red deer bounded away from us as we walked down into the valley. Stonechats called with their throaty clatter. A good footpath, not too badly worn, follows the side of the valley to the top of the headwall of Swindale. A few zigzags down and it's possible to cross a narrow wooden bridge just below the tumbling white water of the Forces, in whose gorge are hidden dark pools and pots, waiting for the tired sweaty walker on a hot summer's day. Over we went and along a footpath that hugs the line of fields on the edge of old deciduous woodland beneath Gouther Crag. Then another footbridge, a short walk on the road, with primroses, violets and greater broomrape, and we were back at the car.

It was a delightful walk, full of surprises and variety in a part of the Lakes that at first glance lacks drama, which is, perhaps, why we had only seen a glimpse of climbers on Gouther Crag and a few walkers in the distance crossing from the head of Swindale to Haweswater. There are many more places like it, just waiting to be discovered.

WILDEST WESSEX
John Cleare

Smooth and verdant down . . . hills and valleys of endless variety
as to height and depth and shape; rich cornland . . . meadows
in due proportion . . . and homesteads and villages, sheltered
in winter and shaded in summer by lofty and beautiful trees . . .

WILLIAM COBBETT, *Rural Rides*, 1830

Four times in my life I thought I was going to die – hardly surprising for one who for forty years has been involved in serious mountaineering over much of the world – and on each occasion there seemed no escape from the ultimate penalty. But, however hopeless the logical prognosis, each time I progressed beyond fear to continue the fight for survival: instinct and experience suggested that that was the thing to do. Two such instances were in the Alps while the most recent was in the Indian Himalaya. But one incident took place years ago and – dare I admit it – in Wessex.

Nowadays Wessex is home. And living there I have learned that although it is essentially gentle, Wessex can be as moody as the Western Highlands. More to the point of this story, however, one corner of Wessex drops abruptly into the sea as a five-mile line of vertical limestone cliffs, which today provide literally hundreds of fierce if fairly short rock-climbs. In the late fifties when we explored these secluded crags with a few other southerners to pioneer the first proper rock-climbs, we soon discovered that there are few easy descents to – or escapes from – the typically wave-washed cliff bottom. Unlike on land-cliffs, safety lies at the top of most sea-cliffs and Dorset was no exception. For the climber, as indeed for the yachtsman, the ambience of the iron-bound Purbeck coast is serious.

With the dusk came rain. The short winter day had been crisp and blue, and the climbing on the white, sun-facing limestone shirt-sleeved and strenuous. Perhaps there was just time to snatch one more route?

But Biven was weary. 'You two carry on,' he suggested, 'and I'll see you in the pub.'

So Barry and I abseiled down to the sea, retrieved the ropes and started working our way back up an impending crack-line towards the cliff-top, 130 feet above. I knew the route – I'd made it myself a year or two earlier. In those days we used aid – a few pegs and a couple of wooden wedges – but we, too, were tired and the climbing became painfully slow.

Forty feet to go. The difficult bit, the light fading fast and the rock now extremely slippery in the drizzle. It seemed a wise mountaineering decision to retreat.

'There's a traverse eastwards along the cliff-bottom to Sub-luminal where we can get out easily,' I explained to Barry. 'I guess it's about five hundred yards. We'll get wet but it's straightforward scrambling and wading.'

'Makes sense,' he agreed, before adding hopefully, 'There's supposed to be a moon tonight.'

It took a little time to descend again to the cliff-bottom. Self-respecting climbers do not abandon gear, especially on a cliff washed in sea-spray, and there were pegs to remove and two ropes to keep from tangling in the gathering darkness. We were too busy to notice the weather. The drizzle had become driving rain as the front swept in up the English Channel. Both wind and tide had risen and white water was breaking over the large boulders at the foot of our climb. It was out of the frying pan into the fire. We had no torch. We were tired and weighed down with gear. We were in a serious predicament.

Initially we tried to control the situation. We would rope up as if we were climbing and move one at a time – each always belayed by the other – wading from boulder to boulder, from sanctuary to sanctuary, working our way carefully along the cliff-bottom. Thankfully there was a little visibility – the night was not completely black – but communication was difficult above the roar of the surf so we determined to keep the pitches short. But the winter ocean is unforgiving and immediately we were soaked to the skin. Wave followed wave, each dashing itself to spray among the boulders or against the cliff-face. On every pitch one or other of us would be washed off his feet only to be hauled back on the rope to try again. My glasses were soon gone. Then Barry was swept from his footing and tossed over and over in the surf, his climbing helmet shattered against a rock. We were cold and frightened. The situation was slipping from our grasp. But we could only go on.

We fought the storm for what seemed hours until eventually I crawled up to join Barry on a boulder larger than most. I recognized where we were. Ahead was the final stretch to easy ground. But it was the crux – the most awkward section. Here the water was deepest. Unbroken by boulders it was unwadable even in normal conditions. The usual way onwards was a strenuous if straightforward hand traverse along a horizontal fault-line crossing the now blank cliff-face some thirty feet up. Alternatively, a rather harder route led vertically upwards to the cliff-top. Now, in the darkness and exhausted as we were, any such technical climbing was out of the question. So could we swim 150 yards – unbelayed – to safety? Without the security of the rope the crashing breakers would make the swim a suicidal enterprise.

Frequent waves broke over us but we'd managed to belay ourselves to our boulder. We shivered until the cold wetness wrapped us in its mind-numbing blanket. It seemed to both of us that that was that. What more could we do? There was no longer anything to fear. By morning we would be dead from exposure.

A light shone through the rain and spray. A rope snaked down, another torch karabinered to the end. It took a major effort to move, then to scramble around and grab it. I clipped in and the rope went taut. With one torch from above, Barry lighting the rock from below, and continual encouragement from a really tight rope, I managed somehow to scrabble my way up the eighty awkward and vertical feet to the steep grass of the cliff-top.

'Reckon you guys owe me a few beers!' Biven grinned. 'But they called time a couple of hours ago so it'll have to wait.

I guessed you'd try this way out. Lucky I had the car keys!'

And then it was Barry's turn.

Thus, most unusually for a mountaineer, I all but received my comeuppance in Wessex. But where and what is Wessex? There are school-time memories of King Alfred and burning cakes, and later, more meaningful inferences from Thomas Hardy, W. H. Hudson and others. But few folk, even locals, can place it precisely. It is not a county, nor does it fit within the modern generalizations of West Country, Home Counties or Thames Valley. Even the BBC disdains the ancient name, preferring to use the vague and ugly term Central Southern England. It seems that only the National Trust and Wessex Water Company (bless 'em both!) acknowledge Wessex as a finite region – a province, even – in the same league as East Anglia.

Strictly speaking, Wessex was the kingdom of the West Saxons which, under King Alfred, rose to pre-eminence in our island in the late ninth century. Though he moved his capital from Wilton outside Salisbury to Winchester, now just across the border in Hampshire, and while actual frontiers ebbed and flowed, the heartland of Alfred's Wessex comprised the counties of Wiltshire, Somerset and Dorset – ignoring Avon as a modern aberration. But, ancient and modern politics aside, in essence Wessex is a geographical entity and surely an aesthetic one. It stretches from the Hampshire chalklands westward to the Brendon Hills, the fringe of Exmoor and the red earth of Devon. It extends from the rump of the Cotswolds above Bath southwards to the English Channel where the cliffs of Purbeck and Weymouth Bay, the strange Isle of Portland and the switchback shores of Lyme Bay comprise one of Europe's more spectacular coasts. Indeed, Wessex is bounded by some 150 miles of coast comprising two disparate shorelines

– the other being that of the low-lying Bristol Channel. Thus, nowhere is more than fifty miles from the sea. Beyond Wessex the land is different. If you have an eye for the country, if you feel for landscape, you will recognize Wessex when you arrive.

Much of Wessex is chalk downland, displaying the firm, flowing lines of scarp after scarp. But there are lush clay vales, wild windy heaths, gaunt limestone plateaux, and the eerie polder country of the Somerset Levels. Essentially Wessex is rural still, an unspoilt landscape of small market towns, ancient coastal ports and pretty villages contrasting the comely and historic cities of Salisbury, Bath and, marginally, Bristol. Victorian Bournemouth, and particularly post-railway Swindon, are considered vulgar latecomers. It may be surprising to learn that Dorset is second only to Northumberland as the least densely populated of English counties, and until the nineteenth century the deep wooden combes of Cranborne Chase provided a lair for outlaws and brigands. Salisbury Plain, much of it occupied by the military but for that very reason preserved from intensive agriculture, occupies a large swath of Wiltshire and thus an important central position.

Here, of course, stands Stonehenge. Indeed the Plain together with the nearby Marlborough and Dorset Downs and neighbouring uplands in Somerset is liberally studded with henges, tumuli, barrows, burials, hill-forts and the enigmatic chalk figures of several horses and a giant. It is criss-crossed by ancient trackways, notably the great Ridgeway and the even older Harrow Way, most still passable if only on foot or bike. Wessex was once the major focus of Neolithic activity in Britain and one senses this ancientness at so many places among these grassy uplands. Stonehenge has unfortunately been desecrated – rendered torpid, in fact – by mass tourism and the motor car, although it is still possible to find the great stone circle deserted, and as spectacular as ever it was, silhouetted against the luminous glow of a frosty mid-winter sunset. The other far larger henge at Avebury, set around a small village, is best appreciated at dawn on a misty morning in spring or autumn. Apart from Maiden Castle outwith Dorchester, huge, well excavated, well documented and much visited but hardly imposing, the great hill-forts of Dorset are comparatively little frequented and typically most impressive. The landscape around the massive sculpted summits of Eggardon Hill and Pilsdon Pen, for instance, the latter the highest point in Dorset at 909 ft (277 m), can have changed little since Hardy knew them, save for the far-carrying sound of the combine at harvest time and the incongruous shape of the modern straw bale.

My favourite local walk traverses the finest hill-fort in Wessex. Indeed, as no archaeologist but as a mere photographer, I consider Hambledon Hill to be the finest hill-fort in Britain. Rising between Blandford and Shaftesbury, it juts from the scarp of Cranborne Chase over the lush farmland of the Blackmoor Vale like the prow of a gigantic dreadnought. It dominates the Vale for miles around, guarding the gap in the hills through which flows the Stour towards Blandford Forum, Wimborne and the sea at Christchurch Bay.

Hambledon is a place where the seasons present themselves in singular guise. In early summer the wind ripples the long grass of its many-fringed ramparts where daisies and cowslips scatter the hollow banks. Larksong and the smell of thyme hang heady on the breeze. The Blackmoor Vale – Hardy's 'Vale of the Little Dairies' – dozes far below, its dappled patchwork of meadows and copses fading blue in the west. Northward the scarp of Cranborne Chase sweeps past the bald dome of Melbury Beacon and the spires of Shaftesbury to Whitesheet Castle, crowned by another fine hill-fort – the final outlier of Salisbury Plain. Further still Alfred's Tower breaks the horizon above Stourhead.

In winter the clouds scud low over Hambledon's prow when the raw south-westerlies sweep across the Vale. The grass is bleached and flat, the wind bears rain in its teeth, the sky and the distance merge into grey murk. Like many a real mountain Hambledon's narrow summit spurs into the weather. Indeed, many a real mountain would envy Hambledon Hill its dramatic situation and shape. All but isolated, a narrow salient of downland rising steeply five hundred feet above a landscape rural rather than wild, it has much in common with the most shapely of Lakeland peaks.

Few mountains, however, can match the all-pervading atmosphere that Hambledon's rich past engenders. On the prow itself stands the spectacular Iron Age hill-fort guarded by row upon row of mighty ditches. No less than three Neolithic camps and two long barrows occupy the airy crest beyond. Here archaeologists have uncovered evidence pointing to ritual human sacrifice. Scarcely a mile distant the path leads onward to Hod Hill, less imposing, perhaps, but famous for the unique military fort superimposed upon its original and extensive British fortifications by the invading army of Rome. Excavations have indicated that the original 'hill-fort' – probably a large, important and well-stockaded village – was reduced by the II Augustan Legion in AD 43, using catapult bombardment. One can only surmise on subsequent events nearby at far more impregnable Hambledon.

Sixteen hundred years later Hambledon saw the last stand of the Clubmen, those ill-starred Wessex peasants and small farmers who opposed the senseless violence of both sides in the Civil War. They assembled at Shaftesbury and dug in on Clubman's Down a mile or two along the western scarp of the Chase but were finally brought to battle on Hambledon's narrow brow. Here, Cromwell's dragoons sorted them out but, for once, with purposely little carnage.

Time has blunted Hambledon's ramparts but, like a real mountain, like so much of upland Wessex, the hill itself is timeless. I love the place – it has ambience, it has personality, it exudes atmosphere. At twenty minutes' distance from home it's fair exchange for many a mere Munro – and one day, perhaps, I shall even climb it on skis.

One summer evening I happened to be driving through the Vale of Pewsey. Rising over the ripe cornfields was a shapely hill with which I was not familiar so I consulted my map and drove up a twisting lane to reach the scarp crest as near to it as I could. Over a stile, a short steep walk led me to the summit where, sitting on the sheep-cropped turf of an ancient tumulus, I looked out through that golden haze of late summer towards the distant scarp of Salisbury Plain. It caught my eye not a half mile distant and some four hundred feet below – a large circle in the standing corn. I'd not seen a proper corn circle before. It was a distance from any lane and would be visible, I surmised, only from here. Common sense suggested it was not the cleverest place to carve out a hoax circle. Two walkers, a man and a woman, toiled up the slope and dropped panting to the turf close by.

'Grand evening,' I volunteered.

'It is indeed,' said the man. 'Have you come to see the corn circle? It appeared last night. Do you know there's one in that field every year?'

'We're corn-circle collectors, you see,' interjected his companion, 'and we're camped just down there – we know the farmer – as we expected one to appear this week but we didn't see or hear a thing all night!' She sounded disappointed. 'This one can't be a hoax, even the farmer believes they're genuine. Extraterrestrial, he says!'

'What do you think?' asked the man. 'Do you think they're real?'

'I've an open mind myself, but I reckon there's more things in heaven and earth . . .' said I.

Believe them or not, it does seem that extraterrestrials take a special interest in Wessex. Every summer the so-called corn circles appear, proliferating across the Wessex uplands especially in the vicinity of Warminster and Pewsey in Wiltshire. Most farmers are sceptical as to their origin and many understandably take exception to what they consider irresponsible vandalism. 'KEEP OUT,' read a notice I saw on a gate near Devizes. 'DO NOT ENCOURAGE CRIMINAL DAMAGE BY MINDLESS MORONS. IT MIGHT BE YOUR CAR OR GARDEN NEXT.' But can the little green men read English? The ancient wool town of Warminster claims the largest concentration of UFO sightings in the country. Perhaps it's something to do with the pre-history of the area. And the consequent vibes.

Another enigmatic Wessex site is Glastonbury where that strange tower-crowned tor rises sharp from the waterlogged, willow-fringed Somerset Levels. Hub of ley lines and certainly a place with as powerful a presence as many a sacred mountain, one can well understand why the mystically inclined frequent it. At one time the tor rose from one of a number of small islands in a wide area of fenland and shallow meres, probably formed during the Ice Age when the drainage of the entire Severn estuary was impounded by an ice sheet from the Irish Sea, which impinged on the North Devon coast. Iron Age lake-villages have been excavated here and birch and alder-slatted trackways have been discovered that linked them through the marshes. This particular island was the fabled Isle of Avalon. Here came Joseph of Arimathea, it is said, by boat from the Mediterranean bearing the Holy Grail – Christ's cup from the Last Supper – to be safeguarded at this already sacred site. The place is steeped in Arthurian legend – indeed, the graves of Arthur and his queen Guinevere were apparently discovered when Glastonbury Abbey, founded by Joseph, was destroyed by fire in 1184. King Alfred is a more authenticated visitor for it seems likely that it was on one of these then all but inaccessible islands, while fugitive from the Danes, that the apocryphal cakes were over-baked.

Just nine miles distant, of course, the last battle on English soil was fought in 1685. The victory of King James II's forces at Sedgemoor, near Westonzoyland in the heart of the Levels, put paid to Monmouth's rebellion. Monmouth himself had landed at Lyme Regis only to be captured a few days after the battle, hiding in Cranborne Chase. The whole business was very much a Wessex affair.

The low country extends eastwards into the Blackmoor Vale where it is contained by the abrupt chalk escarpments of the North Dorset Downs, Cranborne Chase and Salisbury Plain to south, east and north respectively. The Somerset Levels themselves lie between two singular ranges of hills, which run into the sea: the delightful Quantocks on the south, the mysterious Mendips on the north. I like to think of the former range as the final bastion of Wessex before the West Country stretches away towards Land's End. Forming a long narrow whale-back covered in heather and bracken, traversed by ancient tracks and dotted with tumuli, the flanks of the Quantocks are indented by deep combes and hung with woods of stunted oak. This is excellent country for walking, riding and mountain-biking and I'll long remember a recent Sunday evening in the autumn on Beacon Hill, the northernmost top which stands over a thousand feet above, and just a mile and a half distant from, the sea.

Into the westering sun rose the swelling heights of Exmoor, ending abruptly in a steep coast, an imposing and inhospitable shore, worthy I knew of detailed exploration by any sea-cliff aficionado. But to my astonishment, northwards across the Bristol Channel and a full fifteen miles away, the Glamorgan shore seemed close enough to touch. I could count the sails of the dinghies racing off Barry, I could count the windows catching the sunset on the tower-blocks of Cardiff. It was food for thought, and particularly, how varied is the rich geography of our small island, how diverse its scenery.

Windswept, seamed by grey stone walls, dotted with stunted ash trees and riddled by swallow holes, the Mendip Hills form a bleak plateau of karst limestone overlooking the Somerset Levels. The major physical feature is the magnificent Cheddar Gorge, by far the largest and most imposing of several originally stream-cut but now dry chasms incised into the flanks of the plateau. Alas, Cheddar has been defiled by a frequently charabanc-choked motor road, by extensive car parks and by ugly tourist development around the gorge mouth. But in early summer one can still stand ankle-deep in wild flowers on the gorge rim, 350 feet of vertical limestone below one's feet, marvelling at the wide panorama over the green Levels to Glastonbury Tor and the Quantocks. There is spectacular, quite serious and often frightening rock-climbing on the characteristically vertical or even overhanging walls of the Gorge. In fact the dramatic route 'Coronation Street', pioneered by Chris Bonington, Tony Greenbank and myself for television in 1965, has become one of Britain's great classic limestone climbs. But that is another story.

At one time the bleak Mendip plateau was a favourite stamping ground of mine. Tony and I could escape from Surrey early enough on a winter Saturday to spend several hours of masochistic exercise down a pot-hole and yet emerge in time for a pint or two in any one of a dozen cosy Mendip pubs. Suitably limbered up by our exertions, Sunday would be spent climbing at Cheddar or in Bristol's Avon Gorge. Caving was fun provided it was not taken too seriously. We knew no other cavers but we bought a little guide-book, which told us where to find what cave, and we made up our own rope-ladders and used old climbing ropes and discarded climbing boots. This way we explored most of the classic Mendip caves. It was here that I first encountered underground water. In the guide-book the cave was graded 'Severe Pot' but we soon discovered that to competent rock-climbers this meant 'merely entertaining'.

What I found really breathtaking, however, was the underground scenery, its colours, shapes, features and sounds. Far underground a sizeable stream ran down a white-walled canyon-in-miniature and we waded down it. The water reached my knees – I could feel it and hear it but such was the play of light from our lamps and from the white stalagmite which lined our canyon that it was invisible. Then the passage ended abruptly. Our lamps were too weak to penetrate the black void ahead. The stream jetted out into infinite space, disintegrating into an arc of falling spray. A rainbow hung in the light beam. Where else but in a dream can one share utter darkness with a tame rainbow and the thunder of falling waters?

UNDISCOVERED IRELAND
Paddy Dillon

The first time my feet hit Northern Ireland, I hitch-hiked across it from Larne to Donegal on a filthy, rainy night. A week later I hitch-hiked back and stopped off at a couple of hills along the Border. The climbs up the sprawling mountain-cum-moorland of Cuilcagh and the endless, rolling, tussocky moorlands of Slieve Beagh were followed by some frantic midnight hitch-hiking through South Armagh to reach the shores of Carlingford Lough. Not bad for a day in the outdoors. Met some strange people. Got some odd looks. Still wonder to this day what sort of stories are circulating about me. I went up Slieve Donard at a more sedate pace, but only because it was steep and I was wrecked. In those days it was all go, dashing

18

from one place to another, rushing up and down hills and tearing furiously across the most uncompromising terrain.

On another visit I jumped off the ferry and hitch-hiked up the Antrim coast road to walk the Moyle Way. By sheer chance, I was given a lift by a local politician who had sat on the committee that had steered both the Moyle Way and the Ulster Way into existence. He went out of his way to drop me high in Glenariff Forest Park where I could break the law with impunity and doss down for the night. The Moyle Way passed in a blur, as everything did in those days. An overnight ride took me away from the Antrim Mountains and got me in miserable weather to the Sperrins. How I coped with the trek the next day along their broad, boggy, featureless crest in low cloud remains a mystery. This was in the days before metric mapping stretched the whole range across one sheet, and all I had for reference was a motoring map. Somehow, I completed the Sperrins in a heavy day's walk and hitch-hiked away afterwards, eventually bedding down on a dungheap near Newry for the night.

In South Armagh, my intention was to walk around the Ring of Gullion, but the Ring of Gullion had other ideas. Tiny, rugged little hills rose alarmingly from the roadside, covered in the mother and father of gorse and brambles, denying me access at every turn. Climbing up Camlough Mountain above Newry was easier, but that was before the British Army built an observation tower on its summit. In those days, it was just me and a shepherd who had lost his sheep and dog. To cut my losses, I slogged up the steep, heathery slopes of Slieve Gullion and was entranced at the view across tiny fields, dotted with white farmhouses, the Ring of Gullion rising like a circular stockade around my viewpoint. Descending from the hill I set my sights on the rugged little Croslieve, which I climbed as darkness fell. Curious things happen in South Armagh after hours, especially where the Border slices through the area. I disturbed a flock of rooks in a tree and was told to keep quiet by some men who seemed to be smuggling a herd of cattle across the Border. To keep out of everyone's way that night, I slept in a graveyard.

I suppose what I'm trying to tell you, in a roundabout sort of way, is that Northern Ireland is much like anywhere else. I've always treated it that way, hitch-hiking, roughing and slumming it in all weathers. At any rate, that's how I treated it when I had no money. I live a little more luxuriously these days. The first article I ever sold to a walking magazine was about the walking opportunities around the Border between South Armagh and Co. Louth. I was offered thirty pounds for it and it grieves me to this day that I was never paid. To say that Northern Ireland has been a difficult place for me to sell is an understatement. The merest mention of the place would make most of my editors' blood run cold and the subject would be hastily changed.

Once, after record-breaking rainfall, I got off the ferry at Larne and turned right to walk along the Antrim coast road. As I passed the youth hostel at Ballygally, now sadly closed, I mused on how good it must be to be able to afford a bed in such luxury! Fortunately, the next few days were fairly dry: I was dossing down wherever I happened to be at the end of the day. Forging onwards at a furious pace, I covered the whole of the coast road between Larne and Fair Head. Reaching Ballycastle the next day I got a ferry across to Rathlin Island and walked to the western and northern points. Scotland seemed close enough to touch, and I mused that if ever Ireland should sink beneath the waves, Rathlin would no doubt be claimed as one of the Hebridean Islands. Back on the mainland,

I spent an entertaining day covering the whole of the Causeway Coast, marvelling at the complexity of its geology and its amazing variety of landforms. In all the years afterwards, I have never tired of that stretch of coastline. In print, I have called it the best coastal walk in Ireland – and I will always stand by that. My final day's walk along it took me beyond Coleraine to Castlerock and the curious ruined palace and monuments left by the eccentric Earl Bishop of Bristol and Derry. The last stretch of my coastal walk went along a fine sweep of sand towards Magilligan Point. No one had told me about the Army firing range, which was quite definitely in use, but I brought my walk to a successful conclusion.

Another time, in an effort to get to know the rest of Northern Ireland's coastline, I stepped off the ferry at Larne and got another across the mouth of Larne harbour. After walking along Islandmagee I turned round the rugged Black Head and walked round Belfast Lough. While the Carrickfergus shore featured built-up industrial sites and was not particularly pleasant, the North Down coastal path was really very good and people were out walking. In those days I walked phenomenal distances and spent the next day tramping down the length of the Ards peninsula, throwing down my sleeping bag on the rocky point near Portaferry. I could hear people coughing down on the beach, and occasionally shouting out to sea, but it was only in the morning that I realized they were seals.

A ferry plies between Portaferry and Strangford, and crosses an amazing tidal race. Strangford Lough, an enormous sea lough, fills and empties twice a day through a narrow, rocky channel. Watching the boat lurch drunkenly across the channel was enough to put anyone off the journey, but I took my cue from local people, who strolled nonchalantly on to it. The low coastline led around Lecale, with sandy bays and low cliffs. As darkness fell, someone lit a huge bonfire on a beach and as I passed a party was in full swing. Never one for parties, I went on and settled my sleeping bag in a quiet place for the night. There was a rustling in the undergrowth and I came nose to nose with a badger. I said hello, the badger did a double back-flip and charged away like an elephant. My map showed something called the Mourne Coastal Path, but this was really a disjointed series of short paths which I risked life and limb to join together. My walk continued to the mouth of Carlingford Lough, then I turned inland towards Newry, then headed for Flagstaff, Anglesey Mountain and some Border walking around South Armagh.

Gradually, and with no particular plan in mind, I worked my way through all sorts of walks in Northern Ireland. The Mourne Wall was perhaps the most challenging route, following a monumental wall across a dozen two-thousand-foot summits over a twenty-mile course. A week in the Antrim Mountains saw me crossing literally every hump and bump, no matter how many fences I had to hurdle or how many bogs I had to cross. I drew the line at thrashing through forests. I have still not walked around the shore of that enormous freshwater expanse called Lough Neagh: I'm told it is unutterably dull and mostly unapproachable.

People have often asked me if I have ever run into any trouble while walking in Northern Ireland. The simple answer is no. Of course, that's not to say that my walking doesn't cause trouble. I remember an unmarked RUC car following me into a forest once. I was asked a few questions, then allowed to continue on my way. I fared better than the RUC, who were forced to turn their car in a gateway deep in liquid manure. One policeman went in over his boots, and the car skidded, spraying manure all over the windscreen and bodywork. It was a mess, and would no doubt have to be cleaned back at the station, all because I was walking through a forest. One night I was observed by the RUC as I was hitch-hiking, then I was spotted at exactly the same place still hitch-hiking in the early morning. They demanded to know where I'd been for the past few hours, and were rather unnerved when I showed them the flattened grass where I'd slung my sleeping bag. If *I* could lie there all night unseen by them so could anyone.

The soldiers were altogether different, and I tended to meet them only along the line of the Border. They were quite good at keeping out of view, and I often think they only revealed themselves to me when they wanted to. Imagine looking at a stand of trees one instant and seeing only trees. Then imagine looking again at the same trees and seeing fully armed soldiers looking suspiciously at you. Often enough, all the soldiers were interested in was outdoor gear. I've been questioned remorselessly about the nature of my gear, about water-proofness versus breathability, durability versus lightness. One soldier explained how much he had shelled out on DPM patterned Gore-tex, another showed off his flash new survival gadgets. One force I ran into on Slieve Russell had a mean streak in them, and I'm rather glad that their regiment was merged with another because they needed some corners knocking off them.

No matter how much ground I covered in Northern Ireland, there was always the feeling that as an impoverished outdoor writer I was never going to make any money out of travelling around that particular tract of countryside. Editors had no problem with the English Lake District. In fact, they couldn't get enough of it, hackneyed though it was. Eventually I found I could get parts of Northern Ireland into print by piggy-backing them on to other pieces of writing I was doing: with a bit of lateral thinking, it's possible to squeeze a mention of Northern Ireland into any topic under the sun.

By sheer chance, I was contracted to write a guidebook covering all the two-thousand-feet mountains in Ireland. There weren't too many summits to cover in the North and I reckoned that I would be able to hitch-hike my way easily enough from one walk to the next. After a late start Cuilcagh, which straddles the Border, proved energy-sapping and I had to doss down for the night on the bouldery summit cairn. Next day I descended to Florencecourt and hitched away towards Donegal, cutting back into Northern Ireland some days later to cover the Sperrin Mountains at one go. I hitched into the area, crossed the first few summits, had my life threatened by a farmer, continued in mortal fear with the rest of the summits, and finally hitch-hiked to Belfast for the night.

The Mountains of Mourne were all covered from a homely farmhouse B-and-B at Attical, to which I have returned many times. In fact, the Mournes were the last few summits I ticked off for that guidebook, checking routes in rather miserable wet and windy weather. Slieve Donard, the highest mountain in Northern Ireland, was the last on my list, and when I started up it the cloud was tearing to shreds, streaming off the other Mourne summits and being tossed across gaps until there was nothing left but clear views. It was an auspicious end to a splendid project.

I included the Ulster Way in a guidebook that had been intended to cover only mainland Britain. I told the publishers that if I couldn't put routes like that into the book, then I wasn't interested in writing it. That gave me the excuse I needed to walk the whole of the Ulster Way and have some of my costs covered. The Ulster Way was conceived in 1946 as an immense circular route but it wasn't until the 1970s that the route really developed. Then the people of Donegal asked to be included and a separate spur grew out of the original circuit. The finished route measured 646 miles (1,040 km), making it longer than any other waymarked route anywhere in Britain or Ireland. Strange that so few ardent long-distance walkers should have walked it. I think only about twenty had covered it before me.

I enjoyed walking the Ulster Way because it linked together almost everything worth walking in Northern Ireland: the Belfast Hills, the Antrim Mountains, the Causeway Coast, the Sperrin Mountains, the Donegal highlands, the Fermanagh Lakelands, the Border country, Lough Neagh, the Newry Canal, the Mountains of Mourne, the coast of Down, Strangford Lough, Belfast Lough and the Lagan valley. What more variety could a long-distance walker want? Unfortunately, like everything else connected with Northern Ireland, selling the Ulster Way was tough. Finally I was approached to write a small booklet about it while the powers that be tried to decide the ultimate fate of the route. A similar length of walk on the British mainland would have four full-colour guidebooks to cover its length, and there would be plenty of competition between publishers to give it coverage.

Then three things happened, all around the same time, which helped to get a bit more decent publicity for the area. A new walking magazine was launched, and its editor readily agreed that Northern Ireland should have its due space in every issue. The Wee Binnian Walkers decided to stage Northern Ireland's first walking festival: they are based in Newry, enjoy walks on both sides of the Border, and their membership and ethos is cross-Border and cross-community. And there was a terrorist ceasefire. All of a sudden, information about walking in Northern Ireland was in great demand, with magazines tripping over each other to get something into print. I dealt with a few, but it seemed that they were aiming to cover the area only in general terms. Specific features remained solely within the pages of the new magazine and interest in Northern Ireland among British magazines is once again negligible.

The Wee Binnians are a great club to go walking with – but their walking pace is equalled by their dancing pace and most members have taken a solemn vow never to go to bed before two a.m.! They called me their PR man, because I got them into virtually every issue of the magazine. They are probably as well known as any club in Ireland, and they deserve all the credit they can get. Their walking festival looks set to stay and their pace and enthusiasm show no sign of diminishing. They have not only attracted walkers to Newry who would never otherwise have set foot there, but they also go out to other areas and take part in the other walking festivals.

While everyone was riding high on a crest of euphoria following the ceasefires, I was commissioned to write two guidebooks, one covering walks the length and breadth of Ulster, and the other walks in and around the city of Belfast. For the first time in the history of Northern Ireland, there are two full-colour walking guidebooks on the bookshelves. Compare that to the sort of coverage the English Lake District gets – and weep.

One of the problems of walking in Northern Ireland is that wherever you walk you are able to do so only because the landowner lets you walk there. For the most part, walkers know where they can walk without trouble, but occasionally there are disputes over access, raised tempers and legal wrangles. Access legislation for Northern Ireland was framed in 1983, but it was many years before anyone started to use it. Even now, little has been achieved, although Down District Council is a shining example for others to follow. Only in the countryside around Downpatrick will you find Public Footpath signposts where you can follow a route in the certain knowledge that you do so as of right. Other areas are slowly getting to grips with the need for clear access. The offer of money was a great help.

I started covering access issues in Northern Ireland, mostly because people were unaware of what was about to happen. The Departments of the Environment and Agriculture were planning to offer huge sums of money to farmers and land-owners to buy access to their land. Of course, there had to be strict controls and procedures in place, and the access provided had to represent good value for money. Some interesting schemes are already beginning to surface in which members of the farming community are actually pushing their district councils into the access arena.

There's no saying where Northern Ireland will eventually figure in the league table of walkers' places to visit. Even if there were a peaceful political solution to the Northern Ireland question, there is still an inbuilt prejudice against most British people having anything to do with any part of Ireland. You can't easily get round that one, and it's probably not even worth trying. All that really matters is that it is excellent walking country, and there are people who believe that to be true and spend as much time as they can walking there. There's no shortage of walks, and in fact opportunities to enjoy them will probably increase. In the end, those who don't walk there will be so much the poorer. If the average British taxpayer knew how much of their hard-earned money was being spent in keeping Northern Ireland afloat, they would be across there in an instant demanding something in return!

Wilfrid Capper has lived practically all the way through the twentieth century and has seen great changes in that time. When I talked to him, his mind skipped through the decades

– 1916 and the Easter Rising remind him of a trip to Ballycastle in his uncle's car, while a radio was something you bought in pieces and assembled at home. As one of the first families in Belfast to own a television, the Capper household was often visited by friends and neighbours. Wilfrid Capper is held in high esteem by all sorts of individuals and organizations. He was a founder member of the youth-hostel movement in Ireland, helped to found the Ulster Society for the Preservation of the Countryside and has been an active member of a host of others with an interest in the countryside and wildlife. He helped to build hostels in the Mournes with his bare hands, and his group even had plans to 'colonize' the Isle of Man with hostels, but the outbreak of the Second World War stopped them.

It was in 1946 that Wilfrid met the legendary Tom Stephenson and walked parts of a route that became the Pennine Way. Wilfrid returned to Northern Ireland unimpressed by the dreary Pennines, and reckoned that his own Ulster scenery was much better. Plans for an Ulster Way formed in his mind, but it was not until the 1970s that he could interest other people in the idea. Wilfrid was appointed as field officer for six months, which turned into fourteen years, when the foundations of the mammoth Ulster Way were laid. Wilfrid was friendly with the late J. B. Malone, in Dublin, who pioneered the waymarked Wicklow Way. In fact, it was through Wilfrid Capper and J. B. Malone that the notion of waymarked trails all over Ireland evolved.

One of the encouraging things I've noticed over the past few years is the growth in cross-Border co-operation. Some ideas never really got off the ground – one being the twinning of district councils in Northern Ireland with county councils in the Republic: the fact that there are twenty-six of each is no mere coincidence. However, more realistic efforts have been made in terms of walking routes and the great outdoors. The Ulster Way, for practical reasons, crosses the Border in a couple of places, and spur routes have been developed from those points, such as the Ulster Way through Donegal and the Cavan Way from Blacklion. Lakeland Country Breaks in Fermanagh has allied itself with the North Leitrim Glens to promote the scenery and outdoor attractions of both areas. Community groups on both sides of the Border moorland of Slieve Beagh are wondering how to develop the area as a single unit to attract people, and walking routes have been highlighted. The same goes for the Mourne Derg Partnership between Tyrone and Donegal and the South Armagh Tourism Initiative.

There's a lot of work going on to attract visitors to Northern Ireland and the Border counties, and much of the thrust is aimed at the area's outdoor potential. Walkers are best able to make the most of this, and it is sad that they don't come in greater numbers. Meanwhile, the over-promotion of places such as the English Lake District, the Peak District, Snowdonia and the Scottish Highlands is proving disastrous. When I first walked in Northern Ireland few others were walking there, and the maps were lousy. Things have changed. The maps have become clearer and more detailed, more people within Northern Ireland are out walking, and there are more facilities and information sources for walkers – but there has been minimal take-up from the great mass of walkers in Britain.

It's a crying shame, and seems all the more so now, when I have just finished editing a Dutch couple's comments about a walk they made over four weeks around the Ulster Way. 'The people of Ulster are very friendly and helpful,' they say. After walking in more than a dozen countries world-wide they claim that 'the people in Northern Ireland are more friendly and helpful than people in other countries where we have travelled'. One often repeated phrase crops up time and time again in their notes: 'The Ulster Way needs more walkers.' That may be true, but where will the walkers come from?

The Great Wilderness
Richard Gilbert

Imagine the scene. It is a warm day in early summer, you are sitting on a patch of soft turf, resting your back against the summit cairn of Suilven in remote Sutherland and enjoying a panoramic view of myriad hills and lochs and a rugged, indented coastline.

North, beyond Loch Assynt and peeping round the shoulder of Canisp, rises the great ridge of Quinag with its rock towers and pinnacles etched against the sky while in the far distance, just south of Cape Wrath, the sun glints on the white quartzite screes of Foinaven.

A wilderness of interlinked lochs with wooded islands, headlands and isthmuses extends south towards Coigach, where an extraordinary collection of sandstone mountains thrusts up steeply from the bedrock, providing a landscape unique to Britain: Cul Mor, Cul Beag, Stac Pollaidh, Beinn an Eoin and Ben Mor Coigach.

On a clear day An Teallach, north-west Scotland's mightiest peak, characterized by a long saw-toothed ridge, dominates the horizon south beyond Coigach. If you are lucky you might glimpse a shadowy outline of the Torridonian giants, Slioch, Beinn Eighe and Liathach, even further to the south.

Looking now to the west and south-west, three distinct mountain ranges can be seen rising to well over three thousand feet, which provide some of Scotland's most enjoyable Munros. Ben More Assynt and Conival, the Beinn Dearg forest peaks and the Fannichs are more gently contoured than their neighbours but all boast major cliffs and deep, lonely corries. On these hills, where the breeze always blows, you can walk all day over broad, rounded ridges and see nobody.

But perhaps the most exhilarating view from Suilven is to the west. Below Caisteal Liath, the great western buttress of the mountain, lies a collection of white cottages dotted around the sheltered harbour of Lochinver. To the south and north, waves can be seen breaking on the hundreds of tiny islands and skerries of Enard and Eddrachillis bays, a white-painted lighthouse stands boldly on Stoer Point and towering cliffs on the west coast of Handa Island plunge down vertically into the ocean. It is this remarkable combination of grand coastal and mountain scenery that makes the experience of north-west Scotland so exciting.

Why is the landscape of north-west Scotland so diverse? The answer lies in the complex geological history of the region.

Scotland's western seaboard was once the shore and delta of an ancient continent, one of the first land masses in the world.

The base rock is mainly Lewisian gneiss, a hard, crystalline and exceptionally ancient rock formed over 2,000 million years ago. Impervious Lewisian gneiss is responsible for the scattering of tiny lochans, which fill every scoop and hollow in the far north-west, and it rises to three thousand feet on Ross-shire's A' Mhaighdean. Yet throughout much of the north-west the gneiss has been overlaid by red Torridonian sandstone, which was formed in shallow seas about 1,000 million years ago and in places was two thousand feet thick.

The third main series of geological formations was a further overlaying of Cambrian quartzite. This startlingly white-grey rock can be seen gleaming on hills such as Bienn Eighe, Foinaven and the north side of An Teallach. The hard quartzite layer has protected the underlying sandstone from severe weathering, but hills without this protection have eroded spectacularly. Good examples are the stark, isolated monoliths of Stac Pollaidh and Suilven. The Cambrian era also saw the deposition of Durness limestone, which has resulted in oases of greenery and some complex cave systems, particularly in the areas of Inchnadamph and Durness.

A further important influence on the geology of the northwest was the Moine Thrust which occurred about 430 million years ago. Heaving of the earth's crust moved vast areas of metamorphic rock in a north-westerly direction, forcing it over and above more recent rock such as limestone. This tangle of seemingly contradictory evidence was first unravelled by Professor Nicol in an historic paper published in 1859. At the Knockan Cliff, north of Ullapool, the strata can be seen clearly and a visitors' centre and geological trail explain the significance of the Moine Thrust to the layman.

Much more recently a succession of ice ages and their accompanying glaciers have gouged out corries, hanging valleys, deep glens and sea lochs, leaving mounds of moraine and erratics that have been carried many miles from their original mountains. When the ice finally departed, about ten thousand years ago, the earth's crust, relieved of the weight, lifted to give raised beaches, which are very prominent beside Loch Carron and Loch Torridon. The climate became warmer and vegetation spread: Scots pine, oak, holly, hazel, birch, aspen and rowan grew on the lower ground with alder and willow along the rivers.

Although humans have destroyed much of the tree cover of the Highlands by burning, felling and over-grazing, some prime examples still remain. The area around Loch Maree is one of the best for remnant woodlands with oak woods on the north shore and splendidly gnarled Scots pines and other species on the south side. This latter area is now part of the Beinn Eighe National Nature Reserve and receives careful attention. Nevertheless, the original extent of the old forest is brought home to the walker who battles with peat bogs and hags, for bleached roots of ancient pines are often visible when they protrude from beneath the ground.

The dead hand of regimented forestry with foreign species has, thankfully, not been developed to any great extent in the far north-west. Certainly there are many commercial forestry projects, but there is not the blanket afforestation with conifers which is all too obvious in the Southern Uplands, the Grampians and the Flow Country of eastern Sutherland and Caithness.

The very remoteness of north-west Scotland has lessened the visitor pressure for caravan sites, building plots, access roads, picnic places and car parks, and this has helped to preserve its wilderness aura. Estates tend to be very large and the landowners have resisted intrusive developments, preferring to rely on income from the traditional sources of deer-stalking and fishing. For these reasons the vast tract of wild mountainous country between Loch Maree and Little Loch Broom is still a magnificent primeval region which has come to be known as the Great Wilderness.

What can the visitor to north-west Scotland expect? In my opinion Wester Ross and Sutherland make up the most beautiful, rugged and undiscovered corner of Britain. It caters for hardened mountaineers looking for severe challenges in the hills, for modest walkers wishing to explore less remote but worthwhile objectives, and for visitors and families who seek peace, tranquillity and relaxation among the lochs, glens, hills and sandy bays of this unique area.

From Kyle of Lochalsh to Cape Wrath the Atlantic ocean pounds the western seaboard. Tiny caves, broad strands, shingle beaches, broken cliffs, blow-holes, sea stacks, islets and skerries have been carved out by the restless waves over many thousands of years. Inland, beyond the dunes, marram grass and machair, rise some of the steepest and most individual mountains to be found anywhere in Europe. Sea lochs penetrate deeply into the mountain ranges so the sea is ever present and adds a special dimension to the mountains.

Far too many people write off the north-west Highlands because they have heard of its reputation for bad weather. 'It rains all the time,' they are told. But the facts are somewhat different. Cape Wrath has an annual rainfall approximately equal to that of Penzance and considerably less than Windermere. Applecross, further south, equates roughly with Keswick and is much drier than Fort William. May and June are the best months for sunshine in Wester Ross and Sutherland. In this far corner of Britain the weather is often changeable with a brisk wind scudding the clouds across the sky, but this can produce a day of contrasts with an exceptional quality of light and an intoxicating sharpness in the air.

The mountains tend to make their own weather and forecasts can be unreliable. It is even worth setting off in rain, for changes can be sudden and dramatic. Clouds can roll away to reveal black, dripping crags, wreaths of mist in the gullies, rainbows and tumbling burns. If you are lucky you may climb above the cloud into a fairytale world where just the tops of the highest mountains appear above a sea of cotton wool and the sun beams down from a cloudless sky.

Access to the mountains, glens and coastline should not be a problem. A good map will tell you which areas are owned by the National Trust for Scotland, where free access is allowed at all times; other areas are administered by Scottish Natural Heritage and access is clearly indicated. The traditional 'freedom to roam' is acknowledged by most landowners except during the deer-stalking season (roughly mid-August to mid-October) when you should respect any restrictions. Deer-stalking may provide the only income for many estates and is vital to the local economy. The alternative land use might be blanket afforestation, which would be disastrous from an access and landscape point of view. Local hotels or information centres will tell you where and when restrictions apply.

The huge Letterewe Estate, north of Loch Maree, was the first major Scottish estate to reach an agreement with representatives from the outdoor movement. The enlightened owner, Paul Van Vlissingen, signed the 'Letterewe Accord' allowing unrestricted access to the estate, outwith the deer-stalking season, provided that walkers agreed to abide strictly to a code of practice that approximates to the Country Code.

Although I cannot do justice to the glorious country of north-west Scotland in one short chapter, I can describe a few of my favourite excursions to give the flavour of what the fit and experienced walker might enjoy. Ullapool, at the mouth of Loch Broom, is the best centre. Ullapool is a thriving, bustling fishing port for herring, mackerel and prawns, while the Caledonian MacBrayne's car ferry, linking the Scottish mainland with Stornoway on the Isle of Lewis, comes creaming into the harbour twice a day. Boat trips to the Summer Islands in the mouth of the loch are available.

AN TEALLACH – THE FORGE

An Teallach towers above Little Loch Broom, its jagged rock ridges and dripping black buttresses engendering awe in the visitor. The sudden sight of its bare cliffs of Torridonian sandstone rising into the clouds is almost overwhelming to a car driver negotiating the final zigzag on the descent to Dundonnell from the east.

The complete traverse of An Teallach is a major challenge, requiring mountaineering competence and considerable experience. But its position commands both the remote, untamed wilderness of the Fisherfield Forest, which has hardly changed since the retreat of the ice-age glaciers ten thousand years ago, and a stretch of wild coastline extending from Red Point in the south of the Stoer lighthouse in the north. For me, An Teallach provides the perfect mountain experience, from a wander through sylvan woods to high, open moorland, exposed scrambling over pinnacles of sound, rough rock and a steep descent of a rugged glen beside a rushing burn to the welcoming Dundonnell Hotel on the shore of tranquil Little Loch Broom.

After twenty or so ascents, spread over the last forty years, I can honestly say that some of my finest mountain days have been spent on An Teallach: crisp October days with burnished moor grass, yellow leaves on the birch and a sprinkling of fresh snow on the summits; warm days in high summer with fleecy clouds overhead and the aroma of thyme and bog myrtle; frosty days in early spring with cornices ringing the corries and glazed patches of old snow requiring the use of ice axes and crampons. All have provided lasting memories.

I shall never forget the ascent of An Teallach's most southerly summit, Sail Liath, one unpromising day in late October. There was drizzle and low cloud in Ullapool but, bored by inactivity, we donned our wet-weather gear and set off up the Achneigie track.

Half-way up Sail Liath, slipping on the greasy quartzite boulders while freezing mist swirled around, we contemplated cutting our losses and returning to Shenavall bothy to eat our sandwiches and watch the deer. Yet five minutes later, a watery disc appeared in the sky, together with a hint of blue. Almost immediately we broke out above the clouds into warm autumn sunshine.

It was shirt-sleeve order on the 3,100-foot (954 m) summit of Sail Liath. We sat blinking beside the cairn as we opened the Thermos and took in the scene with incredulity. A layer of thick white mist lay over the Highlands to a height of about 2,500 feet. Only the loftiest peaks emerged above the cotton wool, their every wrinkle and fissure highlighted by the intense rays of the sun.

Nearby, across Strath na Sealga, towered the perfect horse-shoe of Beinn Dearg Mhor, layers of fluffy cloud drifting past its buttresses of black rock. Immediately to the west, along the main ridge, beckoned the pinnacles of Corrag Bhuidhe, the spire of Sgurr Fiona and An Teallach's main summit, Bidean a' Ghlas Thuill, streaked with snow.

Later, we lingered on Bidean until the sun began to dip over the Minch. Then, in the gloaming, we raced down through the blanket of freezing mist to the Dundonnell Hotel. It had been a day in a million.

BEN MOR COIGACH: A MOUNTAIN OF MANY MOODS

As the sun sets and shadows lengthen, visitors to Ullapool often drive three miles north to Ardmair Bay to enjoy the breathtakingly beautiful sight of the Summer Isles floating on a mirror sea, set against a fiery red sky.

The romance of west-coast sunsets is well known, but what makes the Ardmair experience so special is the proximity of the great wall of Ben Mor Coigach, which frames the view on the north side of the bay. Like so many peaks in the north-west, the ancient, weathered sandstone gives the mile-long summit ridge of Ben Mor a saw-like appearance. On the south side, the slopes fall away extremely steeply for 1,200 feet and, in shadow, look impossibly precipitous and forbidding. But when the morning sun slants on to the face, bathing the buttresses and accentuating the ledges and scree gullies, the slopes look much friendlier. Indeed, a competent climber could scramble up almost anywhere. The actual summit of Ben Mor lies on the east side of the ridge. At 2,438 feet (743 m) it is a mere pimple by Scottish standards, yet, for complexity and character, it has few rivals.

Behind this great wall of rock lies a whole mountain group, with satellite peaks rising above hidden glens, deep gullies and steep rocks. Broken, vegetated cliffs and tiny lochans abound, and several days should be allowed to explore a wilderness which, with its rich and diverse flora and fauna, is a Grade 1 SSSI administered by the Scottish Wildlife Trust.

The classic traverse of Ben Mor Coigach starts from the tiny crofting settlement of Culnacraig, at the road end beyond Achiltibuie, and finishes at Drumrunie, by the junction of the Achiltibuie road with the A835. A rushing burn, the Allt nan Coisiche, cascades through a deep ravine about 800 feet above Culnacraig. Traverse slopes of coarse grass and heather, and make for the top of the ravine where the burn is easily crossed.

Almost immediately you begin the delightful scramble up a sandstone abutment, to reach Garbh Choireachan at the west end of the main ridge. If you keep to the steepest part of the nose, you can enjoy magnificent scrambling over rough rock, with a fair degree of exposure as you look down to the grey waters of Loch Broom, the Summer Isles and the tiny, brightly painted prawners attending their creels. You could imagine tossing a stone straight into the sea. Whitewashed cottages are dotted along the coastline of Badentarbat Bay while, away to the west, the low outline of the Harris hills can be seen across the Minch. Turn to gaze at the other far horizons: the Cuillin, Torridon, An Teallach, Beinn Dearg, remote Seana Bhraigh and, across Loch Broom, the twin-peaked Beinn Ghobhlach all display their characteristic and well-loved features.

In my introduction I mentioned the special combination of coastal and mountain scenery that is to be found in north-west Scotland; few hills outside Skye and Rhum exemplify this more dramatically than Ben Mor Coigach.

The ridge to the summit is quite narrow in places, with numerous rock towers and pinnacles. You can savour the true crest or take sandy sheep tracks to one side or other which enable you to avoid any difficulties.

From the wind break on Ben Mor's summit descend northwards to the bealach under Sgurr an Fhidleir (the Fiddler's Peak). Follow the edge of the cliffs to the pointed summit of the Fiddler whence, if you have a good head for heights, you can gaze down fearsome boiler-plate slabs to Lochan Tuath, 1,200 dizzy feet below. An easy descent down the wide glen now leads you back to Culnacraig.

CAPE WRATH AND SANDWOOD BAY

The rugged coastline south of Cape Wrath is gale-lashed, pounded remorselessly by Atlantic rollers and virtually uninhabited. Sheer cliffs of grey gneiss, skerries and islets send the waves into columns of spray, with a clap of thunder, wheeling, screaming sea birds and wide sandy bays that provide the walker with a thrilling and memorable experience.

Since transport and communications are almost non-existent in this remote corner of Britain, it is essential to check with Durness Tourist Information Centre that both the minibus service from Cape Wrath lighthouse to the Kyle of Durness and the ferry over the Kyle are operating. The alternative is an extra sixteen-mile walk at the end of an already arduous day. In addition to the logistics of the transport from Cape Wrath, you will need a volunteer to drive your car from the starting point at Oldshoremore, near Kinlochbervie, to Kyle of Durness. However, these arrangements are a small price to pay for the most dramatic and wild coastal walk in the whole of Britain.

From the sandy bay at Oldshoremore proceed northwards, hugging the coastline whenever possible. At times you descend to hidden coves where you startle the oystercatchers and then you climb again to cairned hillocks with heather and eroded peat. The bird life is diverse: fulmar petrels gliding past the red sandstone cliffs, graceful kittiwakes, shrieking herring gulls and superior shags, standing aloof in rows on the rocky islets and spreading out their wings to dry.

At Port Mor there is a beach piled high with driftwood and jetsam. A roofless croft stands by the shore, and a stack of rock, bearded with grey lichen, thrusts skyward, topped by an extraordinary ovoid stone covered with bright yellow lichen (*Xanthoria parietina*), like the egg of a giant prehistoric bird. Further on, as you draw level with the island group of Am Balg, a mile out to sea, the cliffs rise to 400 feet and if you peer over the edge you will see the famous pinnacle of Am Buachaille (the Herdsman) rising 220 feet above the waves. It was first climbed in 1967 by a party led by Tom Patey, who crossed the boiling gulf between the shore and the base of the stack with the help of two ladders.

Barely have you regained your composure after the remarkable Am Buachaille than, rounding the cliff, one of the most glorious sights in Britain unfolds before you. Below your feet lies Sandwood Bay, a mile-long sweep of golden sand bounded by rolling dunes and crashing breakers that make you want to shout for joy. Sandwood Bay is awe-inspiring after a spell of stormy weather when the roar of the waves can be deafening. If you stand on one of the two small tidal islands you can watch gannets diving for fish. Gannets, the most beautiful of all sea birds, plummet into the seething waters, their wings folded and their bodies perfectly streamlined at the point of impact, putting an Olympic diver to shame.

From the cliff top on the north side of the bay you get the best view of all: Sandwood Loch running inland from behind the dunes, a deserted cottage overlooking the loch and the tidal islands where, legends tell us, mermaids play. A Spanish galleon, fleeing after the Armada débâcle, is rumoured to have foundered offshore and the wreck, including treasure, to be buried in the sands. A surviving mariner haunts the lonely cottage where, on wild nights, visitors have reported hearing knocking at the window and seeing a swarthy, bearded sailor wearing a cap, a tunic with brass buttons, seaboots and long gold earrings, peering into the room.

The last six miles to Cape Wrath are exceptionally tough as you switchback from cliff top to bouldery beach, but the scenery becomes even more dramatic. Waves thunder through caves and blow-holes, spray leaps from the shattered rocks and a natural arch runs through the headland at Bay of Keisgaig.

At last you reach the lighthouse with its astonishing power of a million candles, capable of penetrating forty miles of the darkest night, where your minibus transport should be waiting.

Sandwood Bay can be visited on its own, without completing the full coastal walk described above. Cars may be left at the crofting settlement of Blairmore and a rough four-mile track followed to Loch a' Mhuilinn (watch out for red-throated divers) and thence on to the bay. Currently this path is being improved by working parties from the John Muir Trust, who bought the Sandwood Estate for the nation in 1993.

HANDA ISLAND

An expedition to Handa Island is a must for any summer visitor to the far north-west. Not only is it a nationally famous bird reserve administered by the Scottish Wildlife Trust, but the three-mile circuit of the island gives unsurpassed views of cliff and coastal scenery stretching from Cape Wrath to Stoer Point and inland to the superb peaks of Foinaven, Arkle and Quinag.

Handa Island is situated off the Sutherland coast just north of Scourie, less than an hour's drive from Ullapool. The expedition can be combined with a visit to the charming white fish port of Lochinver. Lochinver's new roads, quay and auction sheds are part of a multi-million-pound development funded largely by the European Union.

During the summer months a small, open ferry-boat operates several times a day from Tarbet on the mainland, crossing the Sound of Handa and running straight on to the sandy shore. Handa is beautiful and romantic with plunging cliffs on the north and west sides. Close by the landing bay there is an old graveyard for, before the Clearances, Handa was occupied by twelve families. A path, which has duckboards conveniently placed over the boggy sections, runs across the island to the north coast, passing lochs on the way where divers nest. Quite suddenly the ground drops away leaving you on the edge of a sheer abyss with waves breaking on a boulder-strewn beach three hundred feet below. Rising up from the beach are several stunted rock stacks while, in spring and summer, the air is thick with fulmars, which in recent years have been increasing their population considerably.

A path runs westwards round the top of the cliffs to the Great Stack, a massive pillar of red sandstone completely detached from the main cliff. Thousands of birds noisily contest the nest sites and, if you sit on the cliff top, you will be mesmerized by their aerobatics as they swoop and glide, effortlessly riding the updraughts. Puffins nest in burrows in the thick layer of turf on the top of the stack, while the ledges below make nesting sites for upwards of twelve thousand birds, mainly guillemots and razorbills. Great skuas (bonxies) nest on the moorland of Handa and commonly dive-bomb visitors. The resident SWT warden on Handa walks around in a workman's hard hat!

The waymarked path now runs round to the south side of Handa, passing close to some blow-holes where the sea booms and rumbles in the depths below. Finally, the cliffs give way to a rocky shore with sandy inlets before the path turns back inland to complete the circuit.

I hope I have succeeded in conveying my love and enthusiasm for this wild and exquisitely beautiful corner of Britain. The hills, glens and coastline must be explored on foot, but the walker who makes the effort will find rich rewards.

In the Footsteps of the Giants

Peter Gillman

There was a time when I always did what John Cleare said, so when he told me to follow him and Tom Patey across the moorland from Loch Assynt to the ravined west flank of Quinag, I unhesitatingly agreed. No matter that a bitter wind was scouring the glen, so that as soon as I got out of the car I felt as if I was stepping into a combined wind tunnel and deep freeze. I pulled the hood of my anorak around my head, gripped my wood-handled ice axe, and trailed after them to the point where a cleft in the cliff-face, said by Patey to be an unclimbed route, debouched into the scree.

I was in awe of these people. As a young reporter who had found a way of writing about the sport that already held me in its thrall, I was mingling with its most celebrated performers. Cleare was the leading mountain photographer of the age. Patey, his legendary status already enshrined in Cleare's endless stories, was a demi-god. It did not occur to me to wonder what I was doing in trying to put up new routes with them in the northern Highlands in the depths of winter. On that occasion, after we had climbed the first pitch in Patey's gully, I remember seeing his cramponed soles flailing for purchase on a wall of ice as he battled upwards.

Even Patey seemed deterred. He shouted down, 'I think we'll give the mountain best,' but then, after a brief pause, carried on. I watched with growing trepidation as the minutes to darkness ticked away. I duly made the sacrifice, volunteering to return to the car while Patey and Cleare continued to the top. I tiptoed down Patey's steps to the foot of the first pitch, trudged back across the glen, then waited in the car, trusting absolutely that they would return. It was after nightfall when they did, their faces burning, bringing tales of the gale that had blasted them on the top, compelling them to cling to the heather as the worst gusts roared overhead.

This was my first taste of the Scottish winter. From our base at Ullapool, where Patey was the local GP, I had several other forays into the frozen Highlands that week. On the next, after the slog up the glen from Inverlael, even Patey and Cleare abandoned an attempt on another of those exiguous streaks of ice on the flanks of Beinn Dearg. Then, on one of Patey's twenty-six-hour days, when he kept himself going on Glenmor-angie and amphetamines, we dashed to the Cairngorms, where he escorted me up Jacob's Ladder on Coire an t-Sneachda. Afterwards we drank into the small hours at Jimmy Ross's hotel in Carrbridge – no one seemed troubled that there was a police station close by – until Patey decided it was time he set off for his morning surgery in Ullapool, pausing only to put on his tie when he reached home.

Finally I did my first and only new Scottish route, after trekking through knee-deep snow in Coire Lair to Sgorr Ruadh. Cleare led me up a mercifully easy gully and we completed the remaining steps across virgin snow to the mist-shrouded summit together. 'Well done,' he said, with rare economy of expression.

At the end of the week, I returned to London both appalled and exhilarated at what I had done. I found it hard to believe that I had ventured into such an inimical landscape, defying the wind and the cold, marching across snow-covered glens in a bid to seize the daylight, balancing on glistening ice in my crampons, peering down the gullies as they curved away at my feet.

Then other images and memories asserted themselves. The desolation of Coire Lair, the giant buttresses of Sgorr Ruadh and Fuar Tholl dwarfing our presence. A rippling burn surfacing through the ice. Fantastical confections of ice and rime fashioned by the wind. The mournful croak of a ptarmigan scuttling across the scree. The awe of standing on a summit, braced against the wind, to witness the snow-streaked peaks billowing away to the horizon. They took hold and stayed with me as vignettes from another place and another time.

The years passed. Tom Patey died in an abseil accident on a Sutherland sea-stack in 1970. John Cleare and I saw less of each other on the hill. I did more hill-walking with my wife, Leni, and our sons, Danny and Seth. Danny's first Highland outing was in a baby-carrier on my back as Leni and I explored Glen Dessarry on the edge of Knoydart. We returned to Ullapool for Scottish holidays and together climbed most of the outlandish lunar peaks – Suilven, Canisp, Quinag itself – that lie like sleeping giants along the north-west coast.

For a long time, I had no thought of returning to Scotland in winter: my experiences there still seemed impossibly remote. I did spend a winter weekend in Snowdonia with Ken Wilson, who taught me how to brake with an ice axe and escorted me across the Glyders. I also made a brief February venture to Glen Coe and climbed the Bidean on a deceptive day when the air was still and you could actually get a view.

Then came the catalyst, the dramatic summer's day I spent on the South Cluanie ridge. For twenty years I had sworn I was not going to become obsessed with climbing the Munros, collecting around forty in that time and enjoying hill-walking among the lesser peaks. The South Cluanie ridge changed all that. I amassed seven Munros in a single day and the prospect of climbing them all, although no less absurd, suddenly seemed within my reach. Life assumed a new perspective. Where previously I had made occasional summer trips to Scotland, I now had to get serious. To reach my self-inflicted goal in ten years, by which time I would be in my mid-fifties, I reckoned I would need half a dozen visits a year. And with that time-table, I certainly could not confine myself to the summer but would have to renew my acquaintance with the winter world I had first tasted with Patey and Cleare.

Thus it was that I embarked on my first full-scale winter trip, partnered by Danny, by then in his mid-twenties, working as a school-teacher in Sussex. We chose the southern highlands since they were closest: a mere hour's drive from Glasgow, but eight hours at least for those of us fated to live in south London. There was a daunting start, for we began with Cruach Ardrain on one of those raw days when grey cloud spews across the hillside. The wind strengthened as we worked our way up the hill's western ridge, and then a party of young men, ice rimming their balaclavas, loomed out of the murk, saying they had turned back from the summit ridge in a white-out.

Looking back, I am surprised that we ignored their warning and pressed on. I think now that my outings with Patey and Cleare, even though I followed so literally in their footsteps, must have instilled in me an implicit confidence which helped see us through that first trip. The white-out proved less problematic than the wind, which was roaring around us like a turbine. I could hear my lungs rasping for breath as we searched for the summit cairn, which turned out to be encased in snow. Danny found a niche in the ridge where we nestled from the wind, savouring its intensity, before making our descent.

The rest of that week brought a gamut of raw-edged experiences. We climbed Stob Binnein and Ben More as snow swirled around us, rapidly filling in our tracks. After reaching the summit of Ben More we lost our bearings as we attempted to contour round to the north-east ridge, our line of descent, and heard cracks snaking across the sheets of ice on which we found ourselves. We found the descent ridge at last and felt the relief that comes when you emerge beneath cloud and the landscape opens up like a panorama.

We hit another white-out on Beinn Dorain. It enveloped us when we were half-way up the ridge from the bealach that divides the hill from its neighbour, Beinn an Dothaidh. Unlike on Cruach Ardrain, we could find no rock features at all, and felt as if we were immersed in a white haze, bringing that disconcerting moment when you peer ahead and realize that all you can see are flecks of dust floating across your eyeballs. There was a further shot of adrenaline when we came upon a set of footprints and discovered that they were our own, which meant that we had just walked in an entire circle.

We took a new compass-bearing and, employing a trick I had learned in the Cairngorms with John Cleare, tossed snowballs ahead to determine where the hillside ended and the sky began. We were aiming for a subsidiary cairn at the end of the ridge but found only a single blade of rock projecting from the snow. After prospecting past it, Danny returned and hacked at it with his ice-axe, to discover that it was the tip of the cairn. It proved the key to locating the summit itself, some two hundred yards beyond a dip in the ridge.

We returned to the bealach and headed up Beinn an Dothaidh. We faced another stiff navigational test, as the summit was positioned on the very edge of the plateau, almost certainly corniced and with a steep drop beyond. We were proceeding with the utmost caution when the clouds were shredded by the wind and we could see every step of our route – suddenly so welcoming and straightforward – ahead of us. Danny said it was like waking from a bad dream.

Our last day brought the finest prize: Meall nan Tarmachan, Peak of the Ptarmigan, poised above the picture-postcard village of Killin. The wind was there once again, surging through the glen, but as we gained the lee of the hill it became magically still. A pristine slope gave access to a cirque of rock and ice, its basin carpeted with a rippled snowfield. Danny headed up a gully at the heart of the cirque, ice showering from his axe, the shards glinting as they fell. The wind hit us at the top but we ignored it as we kicked our way to the summit. Around us was a sea of peaks, a landscape of timeless beauty and desolation. Our eyes brimmed with tears as we withstood the wind for as long as we could, before taking the first steps down.

Back at home I knew that I was hooked: not merely on the Munros but on climbing them in winter. Of my next two hundred or so Munros, I climbed almost half in winter conditions, even though this meant contending with short days and climatic extremes. We also saw Scotland away from the tourist seasons, coming to know it in all its mantles and guises. The guidebooks describe some Munros as boring, but in winter that can never be so, for snow and ice invariably provide a new aspect and challenge. With the benefit of new equipment – above all, breathable fabrics – I began to venture out in weather which once I would have considered unthinkable, learning to embrace its moods and testing our own nerve and limits. I learned, too, that this savouring of raw experience, of balancing risk and reward, lay at the core of the sport.

Above all I learned about the wind, never more so than on Schiehallion. It was a bleak February day when it took us ten minutes to summon the determination simply to get out of the car. The wind was soon driving spindrift into our eyes and noses as we worked our way on to the hill's long, distinctive east ridge. We were still below its crest when we were hit by a gust so strong that I was slammed to the ground, as if I had been punched by a giant fist.

The impact of the blow was at first quite shocking: never before on a hill, I felt, had I been so entirely deprived of control. Danny and I debated whether we should carry on, but concluded that, loss of dignity apart, no harm had been done. Once on the ridge we did our best to stay in the lee and reached the summit cairn without further ado. Since then, we have applied the Schiehallion test when trying to judge wind-strength. We ask ourselves if it has actually blown us over. If the answer is no, we carry on.

We learned more about the wind when we set out to climb the twin peaks of Sgurr a'Mhadaidh and Sgurr a'Ghreadaidh on the Cuillin Ridge one April. Although the ridge was in less than full winter conditions, it was liberally coated with snow and ice. After climbing Sgurr a'Mhadaidh we returned to the dip in the ridge known as An Dorus where we made the awkward climbing moves out of the bealach. The wind was accelerating across the crest of the ridge and we tried to reduce its impact by dropping down on the Coruisk side. Although this succeeded, we spent the next half-hour edging along slabs that fell away alarmingly towards the thousand-foot drop into the corrie. It was with enormous relief that we reached the summit but as we cowered below the cairn, watching the hail blasting over our heads like grapeshot, we knew that we faced a similar trial on our descent. We climbed so cautiously that the return to the bealach took as long as the ascent and Danny said afterwards it was the most worrying thirty minutes he had spent in the hills.

On Creag Mhor in the southern Highlands, not even the Schiehallion wind test could help us. It was yet another tempestuous February day, with the wind in the north, and we did our best to find shelter by climbing in the lee of the south-east ridge, which took us to above 2,700 feet on the summit ridge. As we breasted it, the summit loomed tantalizingly close. This time it was not that the wind blew us over: we could not even stand up. The noise was intense and Danny bellowed in my ear that he was going to try to reach an indentation some fifty feet further on. He managed to crawl half-way before pointing downwards. We slithered to the edge of the ridge and dropped down into the hill's southern corrie, lying in the snow until we had recovered our breath.

Finally came the day when we applied the Schiehallion test and ignored its findings. We were climbing the south ridge of Sgurr nan Coireachan in Glen Dessarry, battling our way through a drenching November Knoydart gale. Several times Danny and I stopped to consider whether to continue but once above 2,000 feet we knew we were bound to give it our best shot. As usual we had sought the protection of the lee, but near the top there was no alternative but to move on to the crest. The wind was so ferocious that first Danny then I were knocked to our knees. We were bitterly disappointed, on reaching a subsidiary summit, to discover it was not the real thing. We had even made the formal decision to retreat when, summoning a last burst of adrenaline, we clung to each other and clawed our way to the true summit. We lingered for roughly thirty seconds before fighting our way back to the respite of the lee. We sat and watched the rain sheeting through the glen before carrying on down, both aghast and jubilant at what we had done. At the foot of the ridge was the burn, the Allt Coire nan Uth, which we had managed to cross on stepping-stones just three hours before. Now it was so swollen we had to wade it up to our knees; so buoyed were we by our triumph that we did not care.

We have a hard time, of course, trying to persuade non-mountaineers that these experiences are pleasurable. Privately most of us admit that one appeal of winter hill-walking lies in the sheer perversity of our undertaking. No such caveat is needed on those breath-catching winter mornings when the light casts long shadows across the snow, the air is still and chill, and the sun works its way down the tops. Ben Lawers brought such an occasion, when we strolled along its ridges as if it were midsummer, and spotted an eagle gliding past a thousand feet or more above us, impassively surveying these intruders into its terrain.

On a glowering March day on Beinn Achaladair we laboured through mist assuming that, as usual, there would be no view. A brilliant light began to dance above us and suddenly we were in the sun. It was a cloud inversion, with the peaks around us breaking through like the backs of whales, leaving us speechless – motionless – in wonder. On Beinn Fhada in February, it felt as if we had that giant of a peak to ourselves, working up ravines, passing frozen waterfalls and crossing the glistening summit plateau as if we were the only people in the universe. On Luinne Bheinn and Meall Buidhe I knew I had Knoydart to myself, for I climbed them solo, spending the whole day in trepidation at having undertaken such a major winter walk alone, seeing no one else all day, and returning to Inverie at dusk in utter exultation.

Throughout this period, although I retained my memories of that first intoxicating week with Patey and Cleare, they were gradually overlaid with fresh images. I was also learning to free myself from the thrall of those memories, so that I acquired the confidence to make decisions of my own. And of all the climbs I did with Danny, three stand out for providing vital lessons in winter walking, to do with humility, perseverance and patience.

I had longed to climb Ben Lui in winter ever since seeing those iconic photographs of climbers emerging from the central gully on its great north-east corrie, Coire Gaothaich. Danny and I were with two friends from my generation, Pete and Arnold, who did not want to tackle the gully but were willing to traverse Beinn Laoigh and its neighbour, Beinn a'Chleibh, from the Coire Gaothaich side. We agreed to their plan.

To begin with, all seemed to go well. We were working the two-car trick, leaving one in Glen Lochy for our descent and using the other to get as far up the track in Glen Cononish as we could. For our guidebook, we were following Irvine Butterfield, who wrote in *The High Mountains* that we could take either of the spurs that form the arms of the north-east corrie. The path from Cononish led naturally to the left-hand spur and the route seemed straightforward even as it led upwards into the customary cloud.

Gradually the angle steepened. The route was becoming decidedly more serious, and we found ourselves scrambling among icy buttresses and pinnacles, with space falling away into the mist. At the same time the group was fracturing. Danny was pushing ahead and was perhaps fifty feet above when I realized that Pete and Arnold were lagging behind. Far too late, I scrutinized our map and saw how tight the contour lines had become. We should clearly have been on the south-east flank of the mountain, where the angle was easier. By now we were beyond the point of no return. There was no way of traversing to the easier slopes, while retreat looked intimidating, even if Danny could be persuaded to return to our stance. As usual, we did not have a rope (as a hill-walker, my rationale has always been that if a route is serious enough to need a rope, I would rather not climb it).

I peered once more up the pitch ahead. Since Danny had already climbed it, I reasoned, it should be feasible for the rest of us. The concern was manifest on Pete and Arnold's faces as I stepped up on to the next foothold. It promptly gave way and I slithered back to the stance. I knew this had done nothing to boost their morale but said nothing and tried again. The first moves proved the worst and the three of us eventually joined Danny at the foot of a short but steep convex snow slope. For the first time I realized that Arnold was wearing half-crampons. While Danny cramponed ahead, I cut steps for Arnold into the steepest angle of the slope.

The summit was only a few steps further on but Pete and Arnold were noticeably subdued when we gathered at the cairn. Another party arrived from the Glen Lochy side and were clearly impressed when we told them which route we had taken. Pete and Arnold now announced that they would prefer to miss out Beinn a'Chleibh and go straight down to Glen Lochy.

In the circumstances, Danny and I felt it politic to agree.

In retrospect, the incident fitted the classic mould of accidents caused by navigational errors – the most common single factor in all mountain accidents, as surveys have revealed. Since then I tried to apply two lessons. The first concerns navigation: rather than make blithe assumptions about your route, you should spend the proper amount of time studying both maps and guidebooks – *The High Mountains* even had a photograph of the left-hand spur, showing just how steep it is. You should also plan your route with your companions, so that navigation becomes a collective affair. The second is not to get strung out on difficult stretches, so that the group maintains its cohesion.

We learned about perseverance on A'Chralaig and Mullach Fraoch-choire, my final Munros in Kintail. It was February again, and after we had parked near the Cluanie Inn the line of sunlight was far above us as we set off up the south spur of A'Chralaig. It seemed an age before we reached the sun's first warming rays but once we were on the tops a straightforward walk took us to A'Chralaig's summit. There was more easy ridge-walking to the south top of Mullach Fraoch-choire, but there the ridge narrowed as it dipped and turned towards to the main top. The final ascent contained a section which, as the Scottish Mountaineering Club Munros guide reported, involved 'easy scrambling' along its crest. We both knew from Ben Lui that what counts as easy in summer may be far less so in winter. After both Danny and I had ventured on to some awkward sloping footholds with a serious drop on both sides, we decided – in Patey's words – to give the mountain best.

But when you retreat from a summit, especially one that is so close, it exerts a terrible pull. By then, too, I had become immersed in the mythology of Scottish winter climbing, marvelling above all at Bill Murray's epic account of a Cairngorm blizzard in *Mountaineering in Scotland*. What especially struck me was how he and his colleagues had rejected the temptation to seek refuge at the Corrour bothy on the grounds that it would be 'childish'. Would Murray have given up now, we asked.

As we circled back along the ridge we looked across Mullach Fraoch-choire's western corrie to the slopes beyond it leading to its top. It was easy to persuade ourselves that there was a minimal drop into the corrie and only a slightly longer ascent among the slabs and crags on the far side.

The descent into the corrie, of course, proved longer than we thought, the terrain on the far side more serious. The slope steepened rapidly and became distinctly icy. As Danny moved ahead, I could see most of his soles as he worked his way up among the slabs. When I asked if it was all right, he gave that disconcerting answer: 'I think so.' Finally we reached the crest of the ridge, climbed a short but exposed edge above a cornice, and we were there. The section of the southern ridge where we had retreated looked even more daunting from above. After renegotiating the exposed edge, we had a joyous glissade into the corrie where we sat beside a frozen burn and looked back at what we had achieved.

We knew that by our standards we had pushed it, but the spirit of Bill Murray told us that pushing it was necessary at times. The difference with the Ben Lui débâcle was that we had felt in control and had made considered decisions about the level of risk we were prepared to run. Two hours later we were celebrating in the Cluanie Inn.

The third episode shows how, if you are patient, the hills will deliver you a perfect day. I failed to obtain views from more than half my winter Munros and there were some peaks, as I neared the end of my self-imposed task, that I was determined to save for clear weather. With two Munros and six tops, the Grey Corries were high on that list, for the ridge always looked so elegant, with winter conditions the ideal consummation.

Our time came in February 1996. By now the boy I had once carried on my back was a gentle but determined man in his early thirties, with two sons of his own. On one of those mornings when your voice seems to carry for miles and ice-axes ring out like tuning forks, we set off up the steep northern approach to Stob Choire Claurigh. At first we were in shade but then there was a sun-burst on the ridge ahead and our shadows began to tail us up the snow.

When I first climbed with Danny twenty years before, I had usually waited to shepherd him over the difficult stretches. Now he was inclined to move ahead, but always waited for me at key parts of the route. This time, as I toiled over a crest below Stob Choire Claurigh, I found him sitting beneath a short arête. After asking how I was, he led along it to the cairn. From there we could see the entire ridge extending westwards against a scintillating sky and knew that the day was going to be exactly as we hoped.

We took it slowly, and spent the best part of three hours following the ridge wherever it led, along narrow crests, among wind-blown confections of ice, past snow-covered buttresses and flawless cornices, with the Ben, the Aonachs, the Mamores and other ranges our backdrop beyond. We met two other parties and congratulated each other on our good fortune. We stopped on each top and I took an entire roll of film, usually showing Danny pushing along the ridge, his steps in the snow serving as my guide.

Too soon, it seemed, we were approaching the second main top, Stob Choire an Laoigh. The sun was already dipping as we took the last steps together, but still we were in no hurry. We ritualistically touched the cairn with our axes then sat and looked back along the ridge, now cast in brilliant relief by the light from the west.

'Well done,' I said to Danny, echoing John Cleare's words to me of thirty years before.

'Well done yourself,' Danny said.

THE STRIDING DALES
Mike Harding

You ask me why I dwell in the Green Mountain
I smile and make no reply.
As the peach blossom flows downstream
And is gone into the unknown,
I have a world apart that is not amongst men.

LI PO

Gerard Manley Hopkins called it 'inscape', and though it has many meanings to many people, to me the word carries mostly the idea of a world apart, the inner landscape, that land of our heart's desire that often bears only a shadowy resemblance to the other world, perhaps no more real, of roaring tractors belching out diesel, roads clogged with trippers' cars and wet farmers struggling to mend broken gates with a bit of baler twine. The inner land of our soul is a strange world, a fiction whose narrative is composed of great days out in the hills with good companions and nights in pubs rounding off those days. The other land is a land of mortgages, blocked drains and all the other things that we all have to get through. I have lived for years in both worlds.

My home in the Yorkshire Dales looks out across one of the most wonderful valleys in the world: below my study window the river Dee meanders along what was once the bed of a glacial lake while, far across the Dale, rolling fells lead my eyes towards the Howgills. I can walk out of my door and in half an hour I can be on the shoulder of the crag that rears up behind the house, watching peregrine falcons swoop and dazzle on the air currents below me. Yet further below in the valley the workday life goes on, school buses come and go, the post van stops outside a house – but, unlike Postman Pat, our postie this morning is delivering 'biddings': somebody has died in the village and the 'biddings' to his funeral have been sent out. Yet my world contains at this moment only the fell and those two birds slicing the planes of the air. Behind me the moor stretches for miles to the west and when I turn from the Dale I enter that other world and it enters me. How do I come to be here? Why do I still live here, when, in the last thirty years, I have travelled and walked and climbed in many other parts of the world and could easily have ended up living in any of them?

The answer is complex, and I'm not sure that I understand it fully myself but it probably has at its base the route I first took from my front door one summer's day when I was a kid of fourteen and cycled all the way from the grimy smoky streets of Manchester to the hills of Ribblesdale to begin a holiday that in many ways would change my life.

We lived in a cobbled street, in a red-brick terrace in a city that was then still heavily industrial. At the bottom of the hill was the ICI dyeworks, and across the road from the bottom of our street was the ICI tip where we played, creating a fantasy world from old machines and discarded drums. Years later I wrote a poem about it that appeared in a book for children.

The Dump

Across the tip we played,
Where summers ran screaming
On schoolday's-end legs
And cogwheels gnawed the cinder path
With hungry teeth of rust. It was there that
Gantries looped their smashed and awry arms
And toppled into pools of ebony oil,
Where cables hissed and slithered in the wind.

All those hot summer days of childhood
The tip smelt of oil and rust and grass.
Great boilers boomed like stranded whales,
Their skin, a dry, red, crispy shingle,
That burst into a flame of copper moths
Beneath the bricks we threw.

Then we left them to their dying;
Watched the birds nest in their clutches,
Those cast-off old machines that grabbed the sky.
The fire weed and the ragwort made their way

Through spokes and ducts and sumps
And flashed green rags of banners in the sun.

My playground was a tip,
My countryside a waste of brick and dust,
Where grass and rain gnawed, picked and bit
As the slowly changing landscape fell to rust.

From *'Buns for the Elephants'*

So on that hot August day I left the street and the tip behind, and with a school pal I cycled north, through the old cotton towns of Bury and Burnley and on into the hills where the streets gave way to fields and moor, and the mills fell behind and instead there were only small farms and drystone-walled fields. Just as the children were piling out of school waiting for the buses to take them home we pulled into Settle and stopped for a drink. An hour or so later we were in the youth hostel at Stainforth and in another world. For three weeks I walked and climbed in the hills, cycled the back lanes and high roads and swam in the rivers. I came back many times over the years and eventually came to live here, to enter, you might say, the 'inscape'. Is there anywhere else I could have lived? The West of Ireland is the only other place that comes to mind, though I do find that the Welsh Marches drag me back over and again, and I feel that there is something very deep and special there. But the Dales have been my home for the last twenty-five years, and though I wouldn't claim to be an authority, I have spent a lot of my life there, and most of it in the hills.

It is simply one of the great places of the world. A writer once used the expression 'the Striding Dales', and if you stand on the old Roman Road on Cam Fell you can see the truth in that. To the west the fells march away, rolling towards the sea in tucks and folds of bog and heather and limestone; to the east they stride for mile upon mile over Wensleydale, heading for the gentler lands of the Wolds. Below the striding tops are the Dales themselves, scattered with stone villages, founded by Norsemen and Saxons, and farms like that of my neighbour Billy Mason of Deepdale, whose people have been here for at least a thousand years. All seem to have grown from the bones of the Dale, which in a way, I suppose, they have. Houses appeared on the spring line where the fell water burst out, clean and clear, and that is why in the Dales you will see the 'intake farms' (where the land has been 'taken in' or won from the moor) strung along the fell all at the same height. Villages and hamlets appeared where the rivers were bridged or forded and have grown from a cluster of wattle and daub huts into the dressed stone and mullioned streets you see today.

When I am walking in the Dales, I am always conscious that I am walking not just through today but through yesterday: disused lime kilns point to a recent past while village crosses, medieval trods and Roman roads take us back towards prehistory and the first men here who built their devil's dykes and stone circles on the drier limestone fells.

But to walk the Dales is to walk not just through history but through language too. The old dialect is only a shadow of what it was as recently as twenty years ago, but on market days or at the cattle auctions you will still hear a rough burred tongue that would have been recognized by Chaucer, and by the writer of *Gawain and the Green Knight*. You cross the 'watter' by 'steppin' steans' when you 'gar yem [go home] i' Dent'. And when you walk in the Dales you walk also through a landscape where men have built 'a world from rough stones' and you can see their handiwork all about. The meadows have been won from the rough fell by liming and by walling and, though the walls are not in the state of repair they once were, you can still see the network of the fields stretching from valley bottom to rough top. When I first came to settle in the Dales an old man called Tom Morphet lived in the village of Horton-in-Ribblesdale. He was still talked of as one of the great wallers and in his day had put up hundreds of miles of dry-stone walls throughout the dales. I wrote also of him in verse:

> *He shakes*
> *His head at bedsteads in a gap and rough-*
> *Piled walls, a scrimshank farmer's art. But when*
> *They want a real wall, then they send for Tom*
> *Who'll stand in weather-how and work all day*
> *To make a wall to stand a hundred years*
> *To piece again the pattern of the dale.*

Drystone Waller from 'Daddy Edgar's Pools'

I'm often asked which is my favourite Dale and I always reply that I don't have a favourite, they are all different and they are all special. In Ribblesdale you can walk from Stainforth up the fell to the Celtic Wall and stand looking in wonder at this well-made massive dry-stone wall that goes nowhere and seems to have no purpose and yet took thousands of man-hours to build. Cross the same dale and follow the lane to the neb of Pen-y-Ghent and you can stand on the summit of my favourite Dales hill and look south to Pendle twenty-some miles away and north towards Cam and Wensleydale. Swaledale is a gem of a dale, narrow and deep, the gashes and scars of lead mining still raw on the land. When the lead failed in the nineteenth century, men left here to work the mines in Spain taking their names with them. It is said that you can find, in the Spanish lead-mining villages, people called Jesus Sunter and Federico Morphet. Wharfedale has among its glories Buckden Pike, with its cross and its bronze fox's head placed there in gratitude by a crashed Polish airman who one black night in the Second World War left the wreckage of his plane and followed the tracks of a fox through the snow down to safety.

So many stories – how can there be space here to tell them all? Go and hear them for yourself, go and find the glory.

One of the great walks of the world passes my garden wall. A footpath leads up from the hamlet of Gawthrop by Tofts Farm, once a secret Quaker meeting-house, on by the ruins of Combe House under the scar where falcons fly, and on through Barbondale to the Occupation Road. There you can make a choice to follow the track all the way to the summit of Whernside or cut your walk short and drop down by Flintergill or Nun House Outrake and so back to Dent. This is a walk I have done time and again, and to me it is the very essence of walking the Dales. From valley bottom and river bank by footpaths and bridleways, following packhorse routes that were probably old ways before the Romans came, you claw your breathless way to the summit of a peak to look down at the Dale spread before you. In all weathers and seasons I have come this way and still, each time I make this small but certain pilgrimage, I breathe in the magic I felt all those years back when I pushed my bike into a hedge and climbed, on that hot and seemingly endless summer's day, the gritstone neb of Pen-y-Ghent.

BEYOND THE SEAS OF SORROW

THE ISLE OF SKYE

Terry Marsh

Late one warm spring evening, more than thirty years ago, I first ventured on to Skye and, having neither the time nor the inclination, after a long drive northwards, to go in search of overnight accommodation, I drove on to the stony beach at Camas na Sgianadin and slept in the car. Well, to be truthful, I didn't sleep but sat there swathed in layers of pullovers, a balaclava, woolly mittens and an old Ventile jacket, weary but wide-eyed with anticipation, gazing across fresh blue-green waters to the tumescent dome of Scalpay. For me, raised amid the muckheaps and limitations of a south Lancashire mining community, this was the Promised Land, as Sorley MacLean, the Raasay poet whose work I had yet to discover, described: 'Far, far distant, far on a horizon . . . beyond the seas of sorrow'.

For too long I had been blinkered by urban walls, aware of little more than the immediate environment in which I lived, and knowing nothing of the world that lay beyond. Then Gavin Maxwell's *Harpoon at a Venture* and *Ring of Bright Water*, found by chance in a library-book sale, set flowing the juices of an appetite that has still to be satisfied, probably can never be satisfied, for Skye, the Island, with a capital I, to its people, is a place that defies total knowledge and confounds those who claim to know its secrets.

On that first cold morning, chill dawn air probing the defences of my car, I watched the sky turn pink as the sun hove into the eastern sky behind me, while expectation and the aura of adventure combined to ignite in me a quiet excitement. Suddenly the windscreen darkened beneath the spread wings of a low-flying heron as it glided effortlessly above and down to the water's edge.

Only in my imagination and in films of prehistoric times did such beasts exist, for it might as well have been a pterodactyl, until sense prevailed and a quick study of the books I had with me revealed its true identity.

I was soon to discover that even the briefest of exposures to what Seton Gordon called 'The Charm of Skye' induces a state of euphoria, longing and affection that has come to be termed 'Skye fever'; it is an affliction that not everyone will catch, but for which there is no cure. Perhaps the explanation lies somewhere deep within the elfin lore that pervades the Island, or the keenness of its air, or the edge-defining sharpness of its light, its host of myths and legends, or simply the way it holds a receptive mind for ever in the power of intangible and inexplicable enthusiasms.

Today, if you can ignore the influx of summer tourists from

as far afield as America and Japan, Skye is a peaceful place
that bears the mantle of a modern consumer society with good
grace. But it was not always so, for Skye, as elsewhere in the
Highlands, has grown through a history as turbulent and bloody
as any, when internecine aggression deformed the social fabric
of the Island's culture beyond recognition.

Under the old system the lands of Skye belonged to the
clans, and in return for his support of the chief, a man and his
family could expect to be housed and looked after. But for
centuries this often meant unending warfare, as one clan tried
to gain advantage over its neighbour. That they succeeded,
albeit at a tenuous and temporary level for much of the time,
is evident from the tales that inextricably thread the tapestry
of Skye's history, and the many monuments to long-past skir-
mishes that dot the Island's landscape.

Yet it should not be assumed that the clan chiefs were
altogether a barbaric lot, though none, if the many accounts
are to be believed, was beyond scheming, conniving and the
odd bout of skulduggery. Many, like Alasdair Crotach, the
eighth chief of the Clan MacLeod, were able men, combining
the skills of a military general with those of a diplomat. Alasdair
Crotach was undoubtedly a man of culture, too, encouraging
the bards and supporting the MacCrimmons, the great pipers,
by granting them the lands around Borreraig free of all conven-
tional burdens.

During his time as chief, Alasdair Crotach had occasion to
attend the King's Palace in Edinburgh, much to the conster-
nation of a group of lowland nobility who found the chief's
evident ease in such a grand setting disquieting. When thinly-
disguised attempts to persuade the 'uncultivated' chief to
express surprise and wonder at the magnificence of the palace
failed, one lowland earl, more persistent than the rest, pointedly

asked if he had ever seen on Skye halls so spacious, a roof so lofty, a table as ample and so richly laden, and candelabra so ornate as those in the King's hall. Crotach, in response, invited the earl to see that on Skye there was indeed a roof more impressive, a table greater, and candelabra more wonderful.

When the chief returned to Dunvegan it was not long before notice arrived of the approach of the earl, and preparations were made for his reception. But on his arrival, instead of being escorted to the castle, the earl was taken directly to the summit of Healabhal Mhor, one of two nearby flat-topped summits. As the earl reached the top of the mountain he was greeted by a circle of clansmen all bearing flaming torches, and a mountain top laden with food and wine of all kinds. After they had all eaten, the chief turned to the earl and quietly commented: 'Truly, sir, this is a roof grander than was ever made by human hands; this table, you must confess, is more commodious than any that can be shown even in the royal court; while those faithful vassals of mine are more precious by far than any metallic contrivances, however costly and ornate the latter may be.' In the face of such evident truth, the earl begged forgiveness and tendered an apology to the chief, whereupon the party adjourned to the castle to continue the entertainment for several days. To this day the two mountains are called MacLeod's Tables.

It is with tales such as this that the history of Skye is laden; tales no doubt embellished in the passing of time, but which served to bind the clans long after they were dismantled and systematically discouraged following the Jacobite defeat at Culloden in 1745.

Skye is known by many names. One is Eilean a'Cheo, meaning the Isle of Mist, an unfortunate and inaccurate description

TERRY MARSH

born of a time when mist was viewed in attractive and romantic terms, a misnomer further bedevilled by the publication of a popular account titled *The Misty Isle of Skye*. Another is An t-Eilean Sgiathanach, the Winged Isle, derived from a not-so-fanciful view that the shape of the island resembles some huge bird about to alight on its prey. Rather more prosaically, Skye has been christened the Isle of Enchantment, the Isle of Mystery and the Isle of Fantasy, marketable banners for the tourism spin-doctors. Though valid, they do little to shepherd the visitor any closer to the heart of Skye, the search for which needs more application and determination than brash promotions can yield. One of the earliest descriptions of Skye was given by Dean Munro in 1549: 'The iyle is callit by the Erishe, Ellan Skyane, that is to say in English, the Wingitt ile, be reason it has maney wings and points ly and furth frae it through the devyding of thir lochs.'

Since my first visit to Skye things have changed only superficially, but how sad those changes have been. In 1995, the Island became umbilically linked to the mainland for the first time since the days of creation by the building of a road bridge between Kyle of Lochalsh and Kyleakin. Many of the former single-track roads with passing places have been widened to enable coachloads of tourists to be hurtled from one scenic or historical treasure to the next. All the fascinating, curvaceous and speed-reducing roads have been attacked with a 'Roman' directness that serves merely to speed visitors along in a way that denies them the virtues for which they are (or ought to be) searching – a unique island culture, a fascinating history, a fantastic landscape, and a diverse flora and fauna. Trinket shops, Indian restaurants, visitor centres, car parks, heritage museums, walking-equipment shops, salmon farms and industrial estates have all sprouted where none existed.

Yet in spite of all the brouhaha of the modern tourism culture, Skye retains its dignity, revealing its beauty to those with the vision to see. Today, those visionaries who come to Skye travel in the footsteps of many who have gone before, early travellers who came to study the Island and its people, like Thomas Pennant, who toured it in 1772, and Samuel Johnson and James Boswell, who spent the autumn of the following year touring the Highlands and the Western Isles. When Walter Scott published *Lord of the Isles*, in the nineteenth century, he focused far more attention on the Island than any of his predecessors had, and stirred the imaginations of the Victorian travellers who were to follow. For many years the Island was the preserve of the well-to-do, until the working classes found themselves with paid holidays, and public transport offered its first charabanc tours. Sadly, even today, driving through the landscapes of Skye has come to be an end in itself. Some people, as I do, still come to explore at an intimate level, to feel the good earth of Skye beneath their feet, to absorb the rich atmosphere and the tangled trails that wind across the Island and around its coastline, but so many more seek to 'do' the Island in a day or two, charging about like headless chickens.

It is not from behind the steamed-up windows of a car or executive coach that you will see the real Skye. Take a car, if you must, to travel to the Island's many corners, or use the local bus services, which are perfectly adequate and reach all but the most inaccessible places. Once at your destination, however, the plodding pedestrian way reveals far more than might otherwise be seen.

So where do you find this 'real' Skye?

Everywhere – if you know how to look for it.

And how long will it take?

For ever, if you're lucky.

For most visitors exploration begins as they reach the Island from the mainland. The ferry at Kyle of Lochalsh has indeed succumbed to the bridge, but purists will find the small crossing from Glenelg to Kylerhea, used long ago as the crossing for drovers with their cattle, a way of shunning the blot on the landscape that few Islanders admit to wanting, though the roads that lead to and from it will never sustain a mass boycott of the bridge. Further south, the half-hour crossing from Mallaig is carefully timed to link with the train from Fort William, which in turn awaits the arrival of the overnight sleeper from London and the south. It is a splendid and relaxing way to reach the Island, doing so at Sleat, the southernmost of its sequestered sanctuaries.

The very name Sleat (pronounced slate), derives from *sle-ibhte*, meaning an extensive sweep of moorland. And so it is, an enormous wedge of loch-bearing heather and tussock moorland, dotted in summer with the nodding white heads of bog cotton, and over which common and rough-legged buzzards circle in search of prey.

Sleat was once a place governed by prosperous tacksmen who supervised the management of the farms. From that time one account by Alastair Alpin MacGregor records that 'Slait is occupiet for the maist pairt be gentlemen, thairfor it payis but the auld deuteis, that is, of victuall, buttir, cheis, wyne, aill, and aquavite, samekle as thair maister may be able to spend being ane nicht . . . on ilk merkland.'

But the history of Sleat is essentially the history of the Mac-Donalds, in spite of counterclaims that it was the Irish hero Cuchulain who, in the second century, came to Dunscaith to learn the art of war from Queen Sqathaich. And although for a time Sleat, and indeed all of Skye, was MacLeod territory, by 1498 the castle at Dunscaith was a MacDonald possession, and lived in until the beginning of the seventeenth century.

The first port of call for anyone arriving from Mallaig is Armadale, from where a long and winding road leads up to Strath at Skulamus. But Sleat, often described as the garden of Skye, bears none of the rugged grandeur found elsewhere on the Island, and so gives the wrong impression of what the Island has in store. Otta Swire, whose excellent little book, *Skye: the Island and its Legends*, can still be found in second-hand bookshops and is worth seeking out, comments of Sleat that 'Trees abound . . . every house of any importance has its woods and lawns as in England. The road is bounded in many places with the type of hedgerow which one associates with Devon lanes, hedges of hawthorn, wild rose, and elder.' Boswell, in Sleat at the beginning of September 1773, writes: 'Armidale [sic] is situated on a pretty bay of the narrow sea, which flows between the main land of Scotland and the Isle of Sky [sic]. In front there is a grand prospect of the rude mountains of Moidart and Knoidart. Behind are hills gently rising and covered with a finer verdure than I expected to see in this climate, and the scene is enlivened by a number of little clear brooks.'

Throughout Skye and the Highlands there remains much evidence of that gruesome period in history when greed and indifference purged the land of its people and replaced them with sheep. Known as the Highland Clearances, this unhappy time of forced evictions occurred in the mid-nineteenth century, when almost seven thousand families were moved from their land and sent abroad. Yet at Dalavil, in Sleat, a clearance occurred for an altogether different reason: so that children could be educated. It was cheaper, so the argument went, to clear the crofters than it was to build a school for their children because the community, gathered for generations close by the sea that yielded their sustenance, had no road to it, only a path over the hill. Ironically, if you go there today and think for a moment about how the MacKinnons, the MacGillivrays and the Robertsons who lived in this delightful spot might have felt, you will be saddened by the irony of the intrusive road that has been constructed in recent years to make it easier for estate vehicles to reach the place.

Beyond Sleat lies Strath, which you enter near Broadford. Here is one place on Skye that gives a hint of what you might find on the rest of the Island. Strath is a unique area, independent MacKinnon country, neither North Skye nor South.

Running down Strath Suardal from Broadford, a leisurely single-track road, one of few that remain on the Island, passes the cotoneaster-clad ruins of Cill Chriosd church to reach what must have been the birthplace of Skye. Here, above the reedy, hill-reflecting waters of Loch Cill Chriosd, a knowledgeable eye might detect, on the mountainside above, the site of the main vent of a volcano from which the lavas of the embryonic Island flowed.

Strath Suardal is a spellbinding place, haunted by Ludag, a malignant goblin that might be seen at dusk hopping on its one leg, enveloped in rags, and with a fierce misery in its hollow eye. Loch Cill Chriosd, too, is haunted, by an enormous monster that used to devastate the surrounding land and carry off women and children, to devour them later. Beyond these supernatural spots the road twists and turns to reach the crofting township of Torrin, towered over by the grey ramparts of Bla Bheinn, the first sign of the mountains for which Skye is renowned throughout the world. Inspiration for many poets, Bla Bheinn was considered by Alexander Nicolson, a pioneer of Cuillin exploration, to be the finest hill on Skye. It certainly is a splendid introduction to walking in the Cuillin, and its ascent via the Allt na Dunaiche from the shores of Loch Slapin ranks as one of the most outstanding non-scrambling lines of ascent on the Island, reserving to the very last strides a dynamic and inspirational vision of the main Black Cuillin range beyond.

The Cuillin belong to Minginish (pronounced with a hard G), and are a Mecca for rock climbers and competent mountaineers, a collection of summits that evokes all the emotions. This is no place for novices, and even experienced mountaineers have been known to find situations that intimidate, and conditions that are a law unto themselves. They have been described by H. V. Morton (*In Search of Scotland*) as Wagner's 'Ride of the Valkyries frozen in stone', a not inappropriate view of things, especially when the jagged, gully-riven heights are teased by tentacles of mist, or lashed by the fury of a storm that only Skye could manifest.

The Cuillin dominate Skye, for there are few places from which they are not visible, and fewer sights more moving than when they are viewed in the pink glow of light between night and day from the rise to the north of Sligachan. My own view is that they are seen at their best from Druim Hain, the long ridge that culminates above Camasunary and Loch Scavaig in Sgurr na Stri. From this lofty vantage point you gaze across Loch Coruisk to a great wall of rock, seemingly inviolate, beyond the reach of man. Yet men have climbed here for generations, from the days of John MacKenzie, an early explorer and close friend of Professor Norman Collie, beside whose body his own lies in the old cemetery at Straun.

At the heart of the Cuillin lies Loch Coruisk, described by Walter Scott as 'rocks at random thrown, black waves, bare crags, and banks of stone'. In spite of such adverse reports, Scott's descriptions of the Cuillin and of Skye fired the curiosity of those with the means to venture there. But for me the beauty of Coruisk lies in its complete absence of restraint: it is as Scott describes, a heap of rocks randomly cast down. Here the forces of creation have conjured a scene of wild, invigorating desolation, inspiring countless words, thwarting not a few ambitions, and crumbling to dust many a desire for conquest.

But Minginish is not only the Cuillin. Between the Cuillin, Red and Black, runs Sligachan, one of the most spectacular glens in Scotland; while further north, along the coastline between Loch Brittle and Loch Bracadale, lies a moorland region as fine as any moorland stravaiger might wish for.

Duirinish, by contrast, provides some of the most stunning scenery outside the Cuillin, from the spectacular sea stacks of Macleod's Maidens at the southernmost tip, to the vertiginous cliffs of Waterstein, from where the lonely light at Neist Point marks the boundary between land and sea.

Here, at Lorgill, rows of ruined crofts, their walls still standing against the harsh climate, remain as a clear testimony to the cruelty of the Clearances. Ten families lived at Lorgill, until at noon on 4 August 1830 they were evicted and sent to Nova Scotia, where they were to receive 'a free grant of land from Her Majesty's Government'. Perhaps it is those last three words – Her Majesty's Government – that say most about the inhumanity of the Clearances, for they occurred in Victorian times, an era of enlightenment, some would say, when standards, good and bad, were set that last into the present day. We tend to think of the Victorians as great adventurers and explorers, studious, curious . . . and yet they forcibly packed off their own people in conditions from which 'no appeal to the Government will be considered'.

Of all the places on Skye, Waternish (pronounced Vatternish) must have been least affected by change. One road only runs in and out, compelling those who wish to explore to do so on foot. But the coachloads of tourists, bound from Portree for the castle at Dunvegan, whizz by with little more than a prophylactic wave to the fairies at Fairy Bridge.

Here there is none of the mountain scenery of Minginish, or coastal walking to match that of Duirinish, and the road runs up one side, and that only as far as Trumpan. Yet it is a mesmeric place. In a creek near Waternish Point, Prince Charlie and Flora MacDonald, having been fired upon by soldiers stationed at Ardmore, rested for a while on the Prince's journey from South Uist to Skye in 1746. Along the northernmost tip, two great duns, Borrafiach and Gearymore, are remote enough, among barren moors abandoned to nature, to give a hint of life in former times. Across the peninsula, the twin villages of Geary and Gillen gaze out at the Ascrib Islands and the far green ridge of Trotternish.

Possessing, at Rubha Hunish, the northernmost point of the Island, Trotternish is the largest of Skye's northern peninsulas, and is well blessed with outstanding scenery and interest. From the vicinity of Portree the pillars of Storr are instantly recognizable, and begin the progression northwards of the superb Trotternish Ridge. In turn, the ridge flows effortlessly into the most bizarre of Skye landscapes, the Quiraing, formed by massive landslips of the basaltic lavas from which the area is composed.

Among those who have visited Skye and found only midges, mist, rain, and windswept moors there must prevail an awful sense of disappointment. It is certain that you can spend a whole week of your holiday on the Island and never see a glimpse of the Cuillin, nor a dry day. But when the sun shines and the clouds have disappeared, the magic of Skye is about: its remoteness and peace, its solitude and splendour, its folklore and traditions lay impressions on the mind that are impossible to erase, and cultivate a longing to return at every opportunity.

When I first visited Skye I started by charging off to Portree and beyond, but soon came to realize that such an approach revealed little or nothing about the Island. Within weeks I returned, and, as I have done ever since, savoured Skye's richness at a more leisurely pace, enjoying its atmosphere with the studied, attentive approach one might adopt for a Mahler symphony, for fear of missing some underlying harmony, or a subtle shift in rhythm.

I shall always return to Skye. It is a place where I have found peace and contentment, where I have walked in the past as much as in the present, where the birds have enlivened my days, and the flowers have brought colour and simplicity into my life, where the mountains and coastlines have given days of wandering, and the soft banks of heather endless excuses for lying beneath the heavens and letting the world go by, unnoticed.

The beauty of Skye is there for all to see, but it is not to eyes alone that its beauty is revealed. The charm of Skye is persuasive, and in its charm lies its magic, a magic that will remain long after we are gone.

A KIND OF PARADISE
Rennie McOwan

'Oh, Alva's woods are bonny,
Tillicoultry hills are fair;
But when I think o' the bonny braes o' Menstrie,
It makes my heart aye sair.'

So sang the miller's wife in the village of Menstrie when she was
spirited away by the faeries, stolen from her own man's side, as
the old story has it, one Hallowe'en night when he was sleeping.
She was in a kind of paradise, in faery-land, but her heart was sore
with sadness at no longer seeing the green hills of the Ochils and the
little villages perched at the foot of the steep, southern escarpment
and above rich farmland, which was once mainly bog and marsh.

These villages are called the Hillfoots and are mainly in the Clackmannan and Stirling areas of central Scotland, although the whole thirty-nine-mile long range includes parts of Perthshire and Kinross. Some logical people say jokingly that they should be called the Hillfeet, but local folk have always called these communities the Hillfoots, and that is what is on the indicator signs of the buses.

The ancient Celts called the rampart of the Ochils *uchel*, the high ground, and its southern face, the Ochils Fault, excites geologists. It overlooks a flat plain where there is now drained farmland, the remains of coal mines and the twisting loops of the river Devon and the bigger river Forth. The sea once covered this ground and lapped against forest-clad hills.

The modern hillwalker looks down on farms and roads, which now sit on top of a silted-up plain that contains the remains of oyster beds and where the bones of whales have been found.

In the village of Clackmannan, about four miles to the south of the hills, there is a large standing stone which may take its name from the Stone (or *clach*) of Mannan, a sea god whose full name was Manannan Mac Lir, and who figures prominently in Celtic mythology.

When this area was sea-bound – and the river Forth is still tidal beyond Stirling – he was worshipped by the ancient peoples of the dark centuries and his cult probably ended when the monks and priests of the old Celtic Church first brought Christianity to this area. One of these, a teacher and preacher called St Serf, has the title of Apostle of the Ochils and local parishes are dedicated to him, but not a lot is known about him and he may have been more than one person. Tradition has it that he slew a kind of dragon in the village of Dunning, on the north side of the Ochils, and there is still a wood and grass area there called Daiglen or Dragon's Den.

The Ochils are island hills. They are rounded, grassy and heather mounds with a steep southern face and some rocky sections, mainly on the prominent peak of Dumyat (pronounced dum-eye-at) at the west end of the hills and an outstanding viewpoint, and on the front of a hill called Craig Leith (from the Gaelic, *liath*, grey) above the old weaving town of Alva. The name Ochils should be pronounced oh-chils, with the 'ch' as in loch, and not Ow-kils or Awe-kils, and only as 'The Ochils', not the Ochil Hills.

On the north side the Ochils slope gently into the lower ground of Strathearn, once a royal Pictish kingdom, and to the east they fall away gradually into rolling farmland, although there is a prominent escarpment overlooking the Firth of Tay and towards the city of Perth. They are not spectacular hills, but their all-round views to the farms and towns of Kinross and Fife, and to the plain of the Forth, to the rich carseland of the west, and to the far-off big blue hills of the west and north give them a special status.

Sheep have grazed on their grassy slopes for centuries and provided wool for the weaving of tartan, serge and other cloth, and the water of the little hill burns was harnessed to turn the wheels of weaving mills in the Hillfoots and also for flour and meal. The old hand-looms and water power have long since been replaced by electricity and other modern power, and weaving still goes on in the Hillfoots towns and villages. The local tourism authorities promote a weaver's trail, with information centres in the towns of Alva and Tillicoultry (pronounced Tilly-cootry and known to local people as Tilly, for short). Tartan shawls and other cloth were exported all over the world and the shawls, in particular, were popular with

American plantation owners in the southern States as a garb for slaves: the bright colours made the wearers easily visible. The mills also supplied the Army, and Tillicoultry and Alva weavers crossed the Ochils by the hill passes and sold their cloth to people on the north side, some of whom crossed southwards in their turn and sold shoes and other goods to the Hillfoots folk.

The range is about six to eight miles wide and bisected in the middle by the key north–south pass of Glen Devon and linking Glen Eagles, where the famous hotel is sited a couple of miles back from the hills. Despite the number of stone birds dotted about the hotel, its name has nothing to do with eagles, but derives from Gaelic and Britonic words for a church, or *eaglis*. Glen Eagles once contained a chapel reputedly in the care of another Celtic saint, St Mungo, but it is possible that it was dedicated to this saint, who is also called Kentigern, and who founded the city of Glasgow and he may not, himself, have stayed there.

The Ochils are frontier hills. Five languages come together there, old and 'new' Gaelic, Scots, Britonic and modern English. Some of the local place names are difficult to unravel and an excellent book about them was written by historian Angus Watson and published in 1995 by Perth and Kinross Libraries.

The hill called Dumyat has a Pictish fort on it, and from there the painted warriors who gave the probing Romans such a hard time gazed towards where modern Falkirk now stands and where the Red Cloaks built the Antonine Wall, which they later had to abandon.

The name Dumyat may derive from Dun (a fort) of the Myaetae, Gaelic and Britonic words and referring to one of the most prominent tribes, possibly a confederation, who held lands north of the Wall. Another intriguing name is Andrew Gannell Hill, which has people arguing about who he might have been. Writer and mountaineer Hamish Brown, who went to school at Dollar at the foot of the hills, says he sounds like a character in a John Buchan novel, but the name derives from the Gaelic (*an sruth gainmheil*) for a sandy-bottomed burn. The name Mailer for another hill probably derives from the Gaelic *maol odhar*, dun-coloured mound. It is an absorbing topic and arguments range over the meaning of Ben Cleuch, at 2,363 feet (721 m), the range's highest peak, which may stem from the Gaelic for long slope or stony place (at the summit).

Many people consider that the Ochils, in the sense of their having a marked character, end at the west side of Glen Eagles and Glen Devon, but the map shows them running on and merging into moorland and high farmland, crossed by minor roads, until they finally taper off near the Firth of Tay.

Another main pass, now a grassy track, runs over the hills at this eastern end, the old route from the hunting palace of the Scottish kings at Falkland to the royal city of Perth. This route is known as the Wallace Road because Sir William Wallace, the guardian of Scotland, who opposed the expansionist notions of English monarchs – the theme of the Mel Gibson film *Braveheart* – used this road during a period of guerrilla warfare in the thirteenth century. This high ground in the eastern section of the hills once contained sizeable populations and the remains of many houses can be seen, particularly in sections vanishing under growing conifer forestry, a continuing bone of environmental contention.

The Romans may have used the line of the Wallace Road, and the Robertsons who took part in the 1745 Jacobite Rising certainly did because after the Jacobite victory at Prestonpans, in Lothian, they returned home over this road carrying with them their aged chief, and taking back to Atholl, their home territory, the coach of the defeated Hanoverian general, Sir John Cope.

An attractive short walk from close to the village of Glen Farg follows the line of the Wallace Road over the hills and eventually takes the walker into modern Bridge of Earn village. At the crest of this walk is a spot known as Scott's View because it was there that the youthful Sir Walter Scott, then aged fifteen, halted his horse to gaze upon the view. He was going to a house called Invermay where lived an eleven-year-old girl, with whom he was in love, considered proper in these days. He brought this view into his novel *The Fair Maid of Perth*, and for years people travelled to this spot, brandishing the book, and argued about where Sir Walter actually meant. It is, in fact, a little knoll just beyond an avenue of dead trees where there is a lochan and the ruins of houses.

Glen Farg itself is a prominent wooded pass at the east end of the hills and there is also a pass linking Glen Devon with the southern escarpment town of Dollar, where the striking Castle Campbell, one of the Lowland homes of that great clan, looks down at the town from its knoll site tucked into the hills and at the head of spectacular Dollar glen, which is a miniature ravine. Sir Walter visited the castle and John Knox is reputed to have preached there. Castle Campbell used to be called Castle Gloom, as did a nearby hill, but burns called Care and Sorrow may be romantic inventions. It has featured in a number of films. The soldiers of the Marquis of Montrose and Alasdair MacColla, who set out to win Scotland for Charles I in the seventeenth-century Scottish Wars of the Covenant, bypassed the castle on their way to their great victory at Kilsyth in 1646, but shook their fists at the Campbell garrison and burned the villages below.

From the castle, a pass called Glen Quey, which may take its name from either a Scots word for a heifer or the Gaelic *coimhich*, a stranger, runs through to Glen Devon and then over a rising pass called the Borland Glen, over the crest of the hills and down towards the northern town of Auchterarder. This was an old trade route for the cattle drovers when, from the late seventeenth century until into the nineteenth, great rivers of cattle from the Highlands and Islands crossed the hills southwards to the trysts or fairs at Falkirk, Stenhousemuir and Reddingmuirhead. In the drovers' days one of the main trysts was at Crieff, to the north of the Ochils, and cattle from the Lowlands went over the Ochils passes to that gathering. The site was also used for clandestine political meetings.

That great historian and writer A. R. B. Haldane, whose family home was at Cloan on the north side of the Ochils, noticed a grassy track going past his house and worked out that it had known the tread of thousands of beasts, dogs and men. It caught his interest and he eventually wrote that seminal and much-praised work *The Drove Roads of Scotland*.

Sometimes the drovers chose to use the Ochils passes to avoid paying road tolls round the side of the hills. The Tormaukin Inn, in Glen Devon, and the Sheriffmuir Inn, at the west side of the Ochils, were both originally drovers' inns.

The lowing of cattle, the barking of dogs and the sound of great herds on the move are part of the old atmosphere of the Ochils. Thousands of pounds were promised and honoured on not much more than a handshake and when the drovers stayed on for a day or two to relax and be convivial they sent their dogs home on their own. People at the drovers' inns on the way north would feed the animals and speed them on their way.

The *literati*, too, have known the Ochils. In addition to writing *The Fair Maid of Perth*, Scott brought references to the Ochils into a couple of his poems. 'The Lord of the Isles' and 'Marmion'. Robert Burns toured the southern area, stayed at Harviestoun House, chatted up the women (what else?) and produced a couple of poems/songs about the river Devon, which rises in the Ochils. The poet John Davidson, a friend of the internationally known poet Hugh MacDiarmid, spent holidays at the former spa and conservation village of Blairlogie at the west end of the Ochils, and tried to find peace in the chattering burns and peaceful glens, but later killed himself.

The Ochils also had their own bard, a schoolmaster called J. Logie Robertson (1846–1922) who took the pen-name of Hugh Haliburton and wrote poems in Scots. His book *Horace In Homespun* is on the shelves of most Ochils buffs. Earlier this century the shepherds posted his poems up in their bothies and called them 'Hughies'.

Robert Louis Stevenson spent boyhood holidays at the spa town of Bridge of Allan, close to the western end of the hills, and he and his family climbed Dumyat with a mule, which carried the food and drink. Mrs Stevenson wrote her name on the window of their holiday cottage in Bridge of Allan, and a poem about their ascent, which is now in the care of Harvard University in the United States.

The young Louis played beside the banks of the Allan Water just before it joins the river Forth on the fringe of Bridge of Allan, and the noted Stevenson scholar, the late David Angus, argued that the topography of the banks and some very old trees gave the outline of a ship and possibly put the idea of the *Hispaniola*, the ship in *Treasure Island*, into Stevenson's head.

Angus also argued that, when you look from this spot towards the high ground around Bridge of Allan, and particularly to Dumyat, the topography gives the outline of the map in *Treasure Island*. The wooded Darn Glen, which means dark glen, links Bridge of Allan with the small city-town of Dunblane, and an old mine boring there was another favourite boyhood playground for Stevenson. It may have given him the idea for Ben Gunn's cave in *Treasure Island*. When he attended church at Logie, at the west end of the Ochils, and during his holidays, he heard some of the stories about the witches and warlocks reputed to haunt the Ochils glens.

A prominent crag looks down on Logie Kirk and was said to be a coven for witches. It is still called the Carlins' (witches') Crag. Another warlocks' site was at the now ruined farm of Jerah, on the north side of Dumyat, and it is worth noting that nearly all the witches' sites in the Ochils are linked to little rocky canyons or ravines, tucked away in otherwise grassy and pleasant corners. Historians sometimes ask whether 'dark terrain' played a part in persuading the uneasy that those who lived in or near such sites must have a dark side to their character.

Close to Dunning, on the north side of the hills, there is a monument to an alleged witch, Maggie Wells, who was apparently burned there. Her name is not on the lists of people executed in the witch scares of the sixteenth and seventeenth centuries, but many records were lost. She is said to have cursed one of the powerful Rollo family. Each year the lettering on her stone is renewed and although Dunning people deny all knowledge of this the paint always looks fresh.

Faeries, too, had their place in the Ochils and are commemorated at the Faery Knowe (knoll) at Bridge of Allan golf course and in one of the best viewpoints in the Ochils, Ben Shee, from the Gaelic for a faery, near Glen Devon, from where the far-off Cairngorms can sometimes be seen.

Hills connected with faeries are generally conical in shape. In the old days local people treated them with reverence and would not take turf, peat, wood or heather from them. It was believed that the cuckoo did not migrate, but stayed inside such hills all year. The music of faery pipers was sometimes heard from within these knolls, and close to Castle Campbell, in Glen Quey, there is a little clear well pool beside the path, known as the Maiden's Well. Who the mysterious Maiden was is lost in the mists of time, but the faeries are reputed to have been involved and if travellers sit down beside this well and fall asleep they will be spirited away to a faery kingdom.

There used to be a faery ring at the back of the small hill called Craigomas, above Menstrie, and generations of children would toil up to look at it. It fell victim to an ugly, bulldozed estate track, which altered the drainage system of the hill slope, and vanished for ever.

Although the Ochils are mainly grassy heather mounds, split by burns and deep-cut glens, the home of the curlew and the golden plover, they have attracted the eye of the modern mountaineer, partly because of the rocky sides of Dumyat and partly because of their reputation as an all-round viewpoint.

The range includes nine 2,000-foot summits and to combine them all in a day's journey is to climb over five thousand feet and walk more than nineteen miles. Different permutations are available and the southern glens make handy abort points. A common route is to start in Dollar and go up Dollar glen and into Glen Quey. The definition of the Nine is a 'Donald', a list of 2,000-foot peaks in the Lowlands and first catalogued for the Scottish Mountaineering Club by a Mr Percy Donald.

A steep pull on to the most eastern of the Nine then follows, up a hill called Innerdownie, which has a little stone shelter on it where the drystane dyke builders of the past slept out. It links with Tarmangie (goat's knoll) and White Wisp (holds snow late on) and then comes a sweep down and round to King's Seat, above Dollar, a name that may derive from the days when a royal hunting reserve was there.

From here the walker goes across high moorland to Andrew Gannell Hill, then to The Law (do *not* say the Law Hill because that means the Hill Hill). It is called The Law, *the* Hill, because from the southern side it is very prominent. The Law links with the highest peak, Ben Cleuch. Then it is on to a close neighbour, Ben Ever (possibly 'granite mountain'). The last section is across a little bit of the Highlands set down in the Lowlands, a long stretch of peat bog with peat hags and pools, which merit caution and are known locally as the Moss. The last top is Blairdennon, not far from Sheriffmuir, and walkers can descend to the drovers' inn there or work their way into Menstrie glen. It's a rewarding expedition but it should not be underestimated. In mist, or when snow is on the ground, the area can be a test of anyone's navigation skills because the moundy hills seem featureless in poor visibility.

The Scottish judge, Lord Cockburn, ascended Dumyat in 1838 and was captivated by it. He wrote in his *Journal*: 'I can scarcely conceive nobler prospects than there are from that mountain. It is one of the many places which made us not at all afraid to boast of Scotland, even in comparison with Switzerland.'

The cliffs of Dumyat have attracted rock climbers, and the steep front of the Ochils has resulted in more and more hang-gliders using the updraft currents to launch themselves along with the peregrine falcons, which are also seen in the hills.

Much of Dumyat's rock is very friable. It is mainly volcanic breccias or 'pudding stone', so-called because it looks not unlike a currant cake. Its frontage includes some fearsome scree slopes where jackdaws nest in old rabbit burrows and the scream of the vixen can be heard at night. One huge stone was dislodged by ice and water and came crashing down the hill and went straight through a house in Blairlogie. The house was later demolished and the space is used as a car park where the stone can still be seen.

However, there are a few secure lines among the bluffs and rocks and these have been well explored. One of the oldest of Scottish mountaineering clubs, the Cobbler, held one of its first 'meets' to Dumyat. The club was founded by Professor G. G. Ramsay in 1866 and its aim was to climb the Cobbler, that prominent three-pronged peak at Arrochar, on the shores of Loch Long, and any other worthy hill that could be reached in a Saturday expedition from Glasgow. As befits the gentlemen climbers of those days, they crowned their labours with a social evening of a convivial, but genteel kind.

The oldest general mountaineering club in Scotland, the Cairngorm, founded on 9 January 1899, beating the Scottish Mountaineering Club (SMC) by a short head, also came to the Ochils on an early expedition. They enjoyed themselves on Ben Cleuch and wrote it up in their club journal.

Most of the sound rock climbs are in the glen or gully that splits the two peaks of Dumyat and they contain Raeburn's Gully and Raeburn's Pinnacle, a name deeply respected in the history of British mountaineering. Harold Raeburn joined the SMC in 1896 and was on Dumyat two years later. He wrote: 'Dumyat has a charming assortment of perfectly sound rock climbs, but the mountain is rather coy and the good routes are often hard to find.' He pioneered a host of classic climbs in Scotland, particularly in Glen Coe and on Ben Nevis and in winter. He loved to explore mountain ranges and published in 1920 a climbing instruction book called *Mountain Art*. The same year he reached 21,000 feet on Kanchenjunga, in the Himalaya, and he went to Everest on the first reconnaissance expedition as leader of a climbing team of four, but ill-health dogged him. He died in 1926.

Other than the routes climbed by Raeburn, most of the Dumyat rock climbs were first scaled by J. H. B. Bell, former editor of the *S.M.C. Journal* and author of *A Progress in Mountaineering*, published in 1950. Dr Bell, who died in 1975, was described by the much-respected mountaineer and author the late W. H. Murray as 'the best and most influential all-round mountaineer that Scotland has produced between 1930 and 1950'.

Mountaineers from other lands, refugees or soldiers during the Second World War, tried some of the Ochils rock routes or walked the passes. They included Poles, who were billeted in most of the Hillfoots villages, and Norwegians, based in Menstrie.

The hand of man is not markedly on the Ochils, but every now and again there is a fingerprint. The little hill of Craigomas, above Menstrie, has a clear zigzag track cut up it, which later runs eastwards to the Myretoun hill. It was used to bring calcite, a substance used in the extraction of iron ore, down from two small mines when the Napoleonic wars stopped supplies coming in from overseas. It was taken to the iron works at Carron, near Falkirk, where cannon were made and, particularly, the carronade.

Children from Menstrie who played on Craigomas sometimes wandered round to the calcite mines, examined the rock walls of the small canyons and excitedly pointed out scores where dynamite sticks had been placed. Some thought that the white quartz veins were silver, and took rocks home to their unimpressed parents. In fact, silver was mined in the Ochils in the eighteenth and nineteenth centuries and one of the glens above the town of Alva is still called the Silver Glen. The workings have been blocked off and the silver is exhausted, but some of the Hillfoots parish churches have communion cups made from Ochils silver.

There are also short, blocked-off mine borings on Dumyat and elsewhere in the hills where miners sought copper and silver. They may have given their name to a prominent cave on the front of Dumyat, above Menstrie, now called the 'Sailor's Cave' – which deserves to be given a wide berth because the scree is ready to run and down below are houses and a road – but which may originally have been 'the assayer's cave'. Gold has also been found in the Ochils, including some traces in modern times at the north-eastern end. This has caused some environmental antennae to twitch but so far it has not been found in marketable quantities.

The Ochils are great hills for history and geography lessons. They are ideally suited for children to stand on the high ground and look down at the moors and fields and peel back the layers of history, including the days of prehistoric peoples who placed their standing stones on the fringes of the hills, and later generations who held Beltane celebrations on the mountains, with bonfires and special food, to mark the start of the Celtic new year with its promise of golden days to come after the hard cold of winter. The modern habit of going to the summits of hills to see the sunrise – an unforgettable experience if you are lucky with the weather – is a follow-on from the old Beltane celebrations. Local people go to the top of Ben Cleuch to watch the dawn. It is, alas, not a suitable viewpoint to see the sun coming over the far horizon: there are too many other hills in the way.

Christian worship services are often held on such hills at Easter and congregations of over a hundred gather on the top of Dumyat and even more in Menstrie glen. Christianity has baptized the ancient pagan ceremonies.

Of the many standing stones and similar memorials on the fringes of the hills, two are particularly significant. The first is MacDuff's Cross, sited at the east end of the hills where minor roads link Fife and Kinross with the Tay estuary, and which was a kind of sanctuary. Relatives of the Thane of Fife who had committed misdeeds and who managed to reach this stone were regarded as being on safe territory. Other reasons are put forward for the existence of the MacDuff's Cross and it may have been a burial mound, but a 'sanctuary area' is widely quoted.

The second is near Forteviot on the north side of the Ochils, a historic small village which links with minor roads across the hills. Close to the modern village is the Dupplin Cross, whose future is the subject of an emotional debate. Forteviot was an early capital of Scotland and the intricately carved ninth-century cross was erected by the first Scottish king, Kenneth McAlpine, to celebrate the union of the native Picts and the incoming Scotti from Ireland, which led to the formation of the nation of Scotland. The stone is beginning to weather and the National Museums of Scotland want to take it into their care. But the local people wish it to remain where it has stood for centuries, but protected against the weather or perhaps put inside the local church. The debate continues.

The people of the small communities on all sides of these

lovely hills face a challenging task. They are guardians, charged with passing on the Ochils to future generations with their beauty unimpaired.

Some corners suffer from the modern problems of crowded car parks, too much litter and – a horrendous sin in sheep country – dogs out of control. Creeping conifer forestry has brought many criticisms, but the Forest Authority has emphasized that new planting is now done with scenic beauty in mind and includes no planting close to burns, the planting of fringes of deciduous trees close to conifer plantations, clumps of deciduous trees inside plantations, and no blockage of known routes.

Bulldozed estate tracks up Menstrie and Alva glens caused public outrage, but some have grown in tolerably well. This trend is closely watched.

The old Clackmannan council discussed the idea of a chairlift up the Wood Hill, between Alva and Tillicoultry, but happily this idea was dropped, as was a plan for a visitor centre at the foot of Dumyat.

The water of the clear Ochils burns is nowadays bottled and tinned for export to hot countries, but the installations in and close to the village of Blackford are not obtrusive. Reservoirs to the west of Glen Devon have been extended, but this tends not to be scenically harmful. A voluntary organization, the Friends of the Ochils, was launched three years ago and has a guardianship role.

The Ochils have a way of getting into the soul of people, and it is mainly because the upper plateau is quiet and peaceful so that the walker can rejoice in the sound of the wind in the heather and grass, the far-off sounds of sheep, the clean scents of the hill world, and the chatter of the rills, the little burns, with their pools and waterfalls.

Hugh Haliburton once wrote:

> *What hills are like the Ochil hills,*
> *There's nane sae green, tho' grander?*
> *What rills are like the Ochils rills,*
> *Nane, nane on earth that wander?*

Amen to that.

Befriending the Raven

Jim Perrin

I dreamed last night that I returned to Wales. Not that I have ever left this country – or, at least, not for years. But in the dream, those familiar feelings glowed which for me come in response to this place, and no other. Now, sitting here at my desk, the valley filled with orange mist and peaks all around bright morning-gold, I'm assailed by the memory of emotion experienced at coming back to this place, which is like no other. All roads in my life seem to have led to Wales. The images reel past like clips assembled from life's cutting-room floor, edited out of a film where the narrative always runs to evening, home and west.

Myself on roads outside cities, years ago, setting a thumb against the red sun to beg a lift towards it; or later, behind the wheel, seeing hill-fretted horizons ahead and the clouds, fiery circles, the heather burning across the moor and smoke furling round the moon. Now, there is this view – Snowdon up-valley, sea to the west, the curve of a bay, distant Holyhead. But that's just gilded frame, viewed from my window 1,100 feet up on Garnedd Elidir. It's in composition, detail, execution, that you find the masterpiece, which is what this small country between Worm's Head and Holyhead is for me.

Welshness: its root is in the Anglo-Saxon word for foreign; and there is a foreignness about this country that sets it apart from the other regions of Britain. Some within the outdoor community can view land as a series of listed collectable points reaching a particular height, those ridges forming their convenient physical circuit. Once I met one such, by the little pass between Moel y Cynghorion and Foel Goch, on the long ridge by which Snowdon reaches out to the sea (and what a walk that is, from Caernarfon quay by lanes, by standing stones and meadow-paths with screaming plovers to the dark moor, the high ridges). I asked him how he was doing, where he'd been, but he didn't want to stop. 'Along the Big Dipper,' he threw back at me, over his shoulder, in the nasal tones of south-east England. He didn't know – or couldn't be bothered to use – the names of the hills he raced across, wouldn't have been aware that the hollow in which he found me resting, contemplating, is called Bwlch Carreg y Gigfran, 'the Pass of the Raven's Rock'. I feel less affection for or, indeed, affinity with him than I do with the ravens, sleek and harsh, that crowd my garden each morning, take food from my hand if nothing moves, to bear back to red throats already agape in cold pre-spring in their sprawling nest. He – our hill-racer – forgoes or denies the texture of humanity, history, nature; the raven, as those who lived here in their naming recognize, embodies the spirit of its hills.

On a summer evening, months ago, I'd been recording radio pieces, had left the Bangor studios and all their technological impedimenta behind, walked down the road and taken the path up to British Camp. In my student days it was one of my favourite places. It's discreet, hidden somehow, unsignposted, the ways of reaching it not obvious, at a remove from the city. And Bangor, for all its nestling smallness between the two ridges, is that. I don't know if British Camp ever was a British camp. Even the archaeologists seem undecided, the Royal Commission Inventory of Ancient Monuments referring ambivalently to a shale bank that might be natural, might be man-made, and the single recorded find here of a Constantinian coin. But the place still has distinctive character. It feels as fine and apart now as it did on spring afternoons a quarter-century ago when there were always bluebells in the woods of Siliwen, and, at the end of long afternoons with the irregular Welsh verbs of Miss Enid Pierce Roberts or the medieval Scots poets with Mr David Lindsay, lovers would escape up here and look round at a landscape new then in every particular.

On this evening, sitting on one of the simple benches and gazing out over the Afon Menai to Anglesey, I was noticing what had changed, what had remained the same. The framing of the scene was much as it had ever been: the two bridges, the islands, the brocaded oakwoods and wrack-brown shorelines of the straits, the headlands receding eastwards, the pink sunset glow of Ynys Seiriol's striated rock and the way Traeth Lafan's scalloped sandflats catch the slanting light. The statelier incursions of humanity – those elegant terraces at Beaumaris, the 'rich man's flowering lawns' around Penrhyn and Plas Newydd,

Bangor's squat pier, which seems to be hobbling out over the water supported on Zimmer frames, and the tower of Top College, so stumpy from this angle – all these seemed better groomed than I remembered them, in keeping with the yachts and slipways, castellated grand houses and stark white balconied blocks of flats among the dark groves on the farther shore.

As if to compensate, a rash, or blight, of boxy suburbia was spreading across the ridge of Llandegfan opposite, and the pylons were more obvious now. More unkempt, too, was the immediate foreground – a tangled scrub of nettle and foxglove, spindly birch, gorse with the dry husks of its flowers split open to reveal furry black seed-pods, a litter at my feet of cigarette ends, sweet wrappers, the wire from around a celebratory champagne cork.

I looked up from this human detritus and what caught my eye was a bare, forked branch of sessile oak, streaked with bird droppings, barkless and dead, pointing starkly north. Just at the moment it registered on my consciousness, a raven alighted on it.

In our century and urban societies
we are so unused to encounters with
wild creatures. Compare the modern
Welsh poet Robert Williams Parry's
taut surprise at his meeting with a fox,
and the way it slips out of his sight
'*megis seren wib*' ('like a shooting star')
in the famous sonnet, with his great precursor Dafydd ap Gwilym's laddishly familiar apostrophizing of the same animal six hundred years earlier:

> *Gwr yw ef a garai iar,*
> *A choeg edn, a chig adar.*

(He's a fellow who loves the hens/And stupid fowl, and flesh of birds.)

So there was delight in this tamed setting at being in so close proximity to a creature which is, for me, the apotheosis of wildness. And that sense I have of the raven is not just one of those anti-civilization compensatory impulses like that of Williams Parry towards the fox. It is more primitive than that. Remember the Morrigan, the shape-shifting raven-goddess of slaughter in Irish mythology, and how, in the *Tain Bo Cuailnge* she settles on a standing stone and tells matters to the Brown Bull: of hosts gathering to certain slaughter, of the raven ravenous among corpses of men, of affliction and outcry and war everlasting, raging over Cuailnge with the deaths of sons, the deaths of kinsmen, death upon death, until the Bull, maddened, casts off restraint and rages uncontrollably through the land. Remember the Morrigan's temptation, in the guise of King Buan's daughter, of Cuchulain in the same epic, her seductive guiles and desire for love before his battles with Loch's brother and Loch himself. I remembered them as I watched this wildest of birds, this inhabitant of the wildest places, in perfect stillness from twenty feet away, a distance close enough for me to see the dark brown iris of its eye, the dark grey interior of its bill. And it was aware of my presence as another creature. It began to communicate with me. At first, its gestures were aggressive, the wings drooped on either side, tail fanned, bill snapping, and a guttural, metallic note growled out at me. But then it began to relax, the ruffled feathers on legs and head smoothed down, it preened and pecked at the branch, tilted its head straight up in a gesture of supplication or appeasement, looked away and then looked round again, squatted low on the branch with wings half open and tail feathers held straight and quivering, and all the time with a rather soft and musical rolling call to me, and by all of this I was quite entranced.

But as I watched, and as my mind drifted across the terrible

images of mythology – the prophetess of slaughter, the seduc-
tress of warriors, the washer at the ford – I noticed another
aspect of the bird, which caused it to shift in my perception a
degree away from the surprising but still understandable. For
a thickness of perhaps two inches around its entire body –
head, legs, wings, tail – and moving with it whenever it moved,
was a bright, translucent violet aura. Just that. I have no explanation for it. I took off my glasses in case it was an effect
produced by refraction through their lenses. The aura
remained. I changed my angle of view. The aura persisted as
the raven responded to this new game. Suddenly, behind me,
a blonde-haired woman appeared. The raven flew away, taking
its aura and presence with it.

The woman and I exchanged greetings. 'You must be King
Buan's daughter,' I said to her, and walked away in silent,
puzzled laughter. But this is a prosaic ending, and beyond it
came the phase of making friends with ravens. So that now, in
my garden, the young of last year's brood call from the wire
and feed from my hand.

We were not always so familiar, though I've always known
about the place of ravens, and the presence they bring there.

There is, for example, the summit of Cadair Idris. Perhaps
this is my favourite mountain, though I'm not sure: Brandon,
Shivling, Rhobell Fawr – how are we to choose? Strength of
association might lead me to Cadair, though. And, if so, there
would be the pleasure of starting from Dolgellau. It is the
oddest little town, piled-up and intricate, its grey stone and
plain, elegant style taken from the mountain. Down on it, from
2,800 feet above, peer the summit crags of Mynydd Moel –
easternmost of the trinity of great peaks that make up Cadair
Idris. To linger in the National Milk Bar (an institution in every
North and Mid-Wales town), listen to the playful conversation

and admire the lovely faces of the local young women before setting out on a luminous winter's day maybe for the summits, is one of the pleasures of life. The Reverend Francis Kilvert – surely the most amiable of all our great diarists – did much the same thing in 1871: 'I was very much struck and taken with the waitress at the Golden Lion. She said her name was Jane Williams and that her home was at Betws-y-coed. She was a beautiful girl with blue eyes, eyes singularly lovely, the sweetest saddest most weary and most patient eyes I ever saw. It seemed as if she had a great sorrow in her heart.'

Kilvert took the Pony Track up Cadair by the Rhiw Gwredydd, but there's a better way. Fron Serth – the name means 'steep hill' and it is precisely that – on the outskirts of town leads up into an exquisite region of oakwoods, sheep pasture and little ridges at the north-eastern end of the Cadair range. Tir Stent, it's called on the map – Welsh landscape at its most typical and jewelled, looking out to Rhobell Fawr, which rises with an attractive symmetry from this angle above the valley of the Wnion. An old, flagged pony track runs through it over to the top of the Tal-y-llyn pass, and is a good way to gain the eastern gable of the longest and finest mountain ridge south of the Scottish border. The ascent to its first summit, Gau Graig, is a merciless 1,100 feet in the space of half a mile. The view opens out to the north and east with every foot gained. There is a steep and gravelly 500 feet of ascent from Gau Graig up to the ridge's next tier at Mynydd Moel. When last here, I was dawdling up it as a friendly sheepdog came bounding down with two walkers in attendance, heading for the valley with huge sacks, on which were strapped ice-axes and crampons, though not so much as a rag or shred of snow was to be seen, even in the most northerly of gullies. They gave me a breezy, stern hello and strode off purposefully after the dog, who seemed as impatient at their progress as they were dismissive of mine. Within a few minutes I was on top of Mynydd Moel, with the world and its people scattering off in all directions.

If you have never been up Cadair from this eastern end then you have a delight in store. From the state of the paths, by far the greater number who do climb Cadair seem never to venture even so far as Mynydd Moel, which is a great hill in its own right, massive in presence as you approach it from the east. Its top is particularly fine, with a shelter-cairn and a little cockscomb of rocks above plunging crags. You can see from it straight down on to Dolgellau, a bare two miles away, and that gives you the clue as to why, in Elizabethan times, this was considered the highest mountain in the British Isles. Penygadair – highest point of the Cadair range – may only be 2,928 feet (892 m) above sea level, but sea level is just down there. Dolgellau is at it. Ben Nevis may be half as high again but it is twice as far from the sea. Those sandflats and long, low saltings of the Mawddach estuary give Cadair its uplift, its subjective impression of height. It *feels* a tremendous mountain.

And I'm tempted to state that Mynydd Moel is the best part of it. Even its name suggests the effect it has, translating loosely as 'the Mountain Mountain', in a deliberately intensifying way. From it, you look right along the northern escarpment, lakes flashing silver from glaciated hollows around which elegant ridges glint skywards. Walk a few yards down the southern slope and you're confronted by a view a version of which is one of the masterpieces of eighteenth-century art. Richard Wilson's *Cadar Idris, Lyn-y-cau* of 1765 is one of those paintings that anyone with a vestige of interest in art knows. It's in the Tate in London and I go to see it there when I can – a surprisingly small canvas, not much more than eighteen inches high by two feet or so wide, all russets and Payne's grey with the palest blues and greens and a touch of gold on foreground boulders, which root its conceptual diagonals firmly in the landscape. It always shocks me with its capacity simultaneously to be like and yet unlike. It's less the depiction of a mountain scene than its reordering, the interpretation of its essence by a man with a kindly, respectful and loving view of nature and its power for harmony. I love it, and the place it so wonderfully expresses.

If Richard Wilson had seen it on a day like the one I was enjoying, his painting might have been even more haunting and suffused with the golden light of a Claude landscape instead of its merest suggestion. I've seldom seen so far from the hills: Snowdon seemed almost within touching distance to the north, and Snaefell hung like a cloud behind it, while to the south-east and the south-west the Malvern Hills and the Preselis delimited the horizon, so clear that their every summit was identifiable. Only to the west was the clarity compromised by an encroaching heavy front that moved inexorably in through the course of the afternoon. A blustery wind scoured the plateau between Mynydd Moel and Penygadair. Two walkers surfing along on it stopped to talk excitedly of the day's quality, their speech gasping and fragmented: 'Perfect . . . the views . . . can see everything . . . oh!' One of them recognized me from a time we had worked together on nightshifts in a Caernarfon factory nearly thirty years ago, making upholstery for cars that will all long since have gone to the scrap-heap, and neither of us knowing then of the other's passion for these enduring places. I left them to climb on to the summit, and all the memories that place holds for me. And as I arrived, the ravens grated their welcome.

These birds and their parents I have known for forty years. This was the first mountain I climbed in Wales, in that burnished summer at the end of the 1950s, and they were there then, tumbling joyful acrobats around the summit whose flight spelt freedom, but whose presence was a strange longing, the exact words for which remain fixed only in feeling, refusing ever to succumb to our quest for definition, the birds haunting the mirror tunnels of memory. Tilman is one of them now, whom I first met here, and my younger self, too, soloing up the Cyfrwy Arête in the wind's exuberance. If I could never return, each bird would dance a memory there for me, memory being our slow descent from the summit-present, from the cold shelter hut I inhabit there.

Outside, wind freezes fingers and cheekbones in an instant, and I shuffle rapidly down to Cyfrwy. It must have been from here that on his ascent Kilvert's guide pointed out the place 'at the foot of an opposite precipice' where the body of the unfortunate Mr Smith had been found. He was a clerk from Newport on a walking tour of Wales in September 1865, who had disappeared while attempting to traverse the mountain in poor weather and darkness without a guide. He was found the following May: 'The foxes and ravens had eaten him. His eyes were gone. His teeth were dashed out by the fall and lay scattered about on the mountain . . .' I was glad to pass on and race down the broad ridge over Rhiw Gwredydd, where the ponies once climbed up from the Dysynni valley, and on past Tyrau Mawr to Braich Ddu, the ridge's unvisited seaward gable, which I descended in the gathering dark with the light of Ynys Enlli flashing thirty miles across the bay. The vague path mis-led me into young spruce plantation, and on to the grimiest forestry track I've ever had the misfortune to stumble along. But by Cyfannedd a gibbous moon cast latticed shadows of branches across the road, an owl's wavering scream tore at the woods' silence, curlews descanted in the estuary. I took the footpath across the Barmouth rail-bridge, with slick, black water running fast beneath, between the baulks the shipworm gnaws, and I thought of poor Kilvert and his proper yearnings again: 'I have always had a vision of coming into a Welsh town above sunset and seeing the children playing on the bridge and this evening the dream came true.' If they had only been his, and his had been a satisfied life, sweet soul that he was. But maybe to ask for more than glimpses and memories of the perfect state is to ask too much. Maybe only in moments – as accessible in the mountains' simplicity as anywhere – does the landscape of our life approach the harmony of Richard Wilson's vision.

As with another time, beneath Clogwyn Du'r Arddu. I am listening to the raven's metallic call, echoing around the crags, and I am quite alone on a still, dry autumn day. I love this cliff – its tilting symmetries, its soar, its silvered rock. In architecture, atmosphere and detail, there's none finer in Britain. I'm in my climber's prime – strong, slim and confident so that the moves slip by and clean my soles on the shattered boss of rock by which the White Slab starts. Slaty-smooth, delaminating holds lead across, above is grass and a little safe corner to hide in before the long pitches start. I step into the journey. To the left of these leaning slabs, everything falls away, but space is no more than threat and consequence, and reality's in the fingers' grip on sharp, sound tiny holds, in the careful-angled foot whose sole the same will bite. Beyond fear, so many moves to string together, the calm elation comes. You live on the brink of laughter. How ambiguous would be the falling scream? I trail a rope tied loosely round my waist, because this trip's for pleasure, not achievement. There is a lasso pitch, the alternative too hard for relaxation. But after, on the last long slab, the raven perches near to me, eyeing with cocked head the trailing line as though it were some monstrous worm.

My dark and cosmic friend . . .

In a churchyard, high up in rocky bluffs on a shoulder of Tal y Fan, I sit among graves. Its name is Llangelynin – the old church, not the new – and it dates from the twelfth century. But it's essentially timeless, low and sturdy in its walled enclosure with the earth heaving and swelling against it. Inside, all is unerring simplicity. The north transept is a *capel y meibion* (men's chapel). When I was last here a mole had thrown up a mound of soil from between the flags of the floor in chthonic jest. Painted on the east wall are the Commandments and the Lord's Prayer, in Welsh and dating from the Restoration. In the churchyard, ash and hawthorn grow from a sheltering bank, the graves of the unnamed and the named mingle, the epitaphs on the latter expressing a sense of the place. The south-west corner has a well, Ffynnon Gelynin – a stone *cist* in a thick-walled enclosure, formerly roofed-over, which was supposed to have the power of divination. Clothes of sick children were placed in the water: if they floated, the child would live. It's scummy with algal growth and infested with pond-skaters now. Invested magic gone, nettles and ferns grow from its walls. The anxieties and miseries enacted here are forgotten and unmarked by anything but the small, harebell-crested mounds of minimal record in which the churchyard abounds, the significance of which is salutary to those who see here only peace.

There are few places I know that are more Welsh, more particular to these hills and reflective of their history, nature, community. A young woman creaks the gate, nods and smiles, goes into the church. After a while she emerges again and comes across to where I lie at rest. She talks to me: of having lived in London, been unhappy there, thought often of this place. On a pillowy grave, a greensward mattress of unnumbered bones, we lie and talk, and if desire flickers between us, as play of word and gesture intimates, it is not stated, not urgent. At length, lingeringly, she goes, and I, who am lazy and peaceful in the sun, remain on the greensward, and keep so still that when his pinions hiss, as he alights and grips the edge of stone his eye fixes my immobility. He cranes his head sidelong to view. Am I his prey? He cranes his head and seems to read words written on stone:

'Who shall dwell in thy holy hill?'

Only the raven's friend . . .

Greensand Roots

Kev Reynolds

Pity the nomad who has no roots, no sense of belonging to any one particular place, no emotional tie to the land. That nomad may drift from one horizon to another and feel only a compulsion to keep moving; a restless impulse, a lifelong search – but for what? Towards what? Away from what? There is, it may be argued – and who am I to deny it? – a romance in that very restlessness, an anarchic spirit that rises up and refuses to be anchored, fearful perhaps of being sucked into the sin of conformity, uniformity, the deadening monotony of sameness.

But the wandering star that guides and directs and refuses to settle ensures that the wanderer gathers nothing but transitory impressions of the world through which he travels, is left with a kaleidoscopic memory alone, a fragmented picture of a series of landscapes, incomplete and ephemeral. Nothing wrong with that, of course, but how much better it is to have both the drift *and* a base; the freedom of movement alive with the mystery of distant lands, *and* the knowledge that there awaits at the end of each journey a landscape that spells home, with all the certain reassurance a countryman needs.

Such a place to me is Greensand Country.

The Greensand Ridge forms an inner lining to the great chalk escarpment of the North Downs. Better by far than the Downs, Greensand Country embraces the lush acres of the Weald, that Roman forested wilderness of *Anderida* that was destined to become the very garden of England. Easing through Surrey and across much of Kent this ridge arcs in an extensive line of hills, crowned with beechwoods here, silver with birches there, fronded with open heath and deer-grazed meadow – and always, always it seems, with one jutting prow after another providing viewpoints to warm the heart of anyone capable of being stirred by nature's abundant goodness. This is, after all, a countryman's country. Not wilderness, not the dramatic undulation of raw rock and glacier, but a lowland country, productive, benevolent, rewarding. A landscape to care for, to bless and be blessed by. And it is the land I scurry home to from expeditions remote and wild.

Transplanted roots take time to firm themselves into the earth. Not so mine. I came here teased by prospects of work, having been wrenched from mountains that had, I'd once thought, meant everything. Or nearly everything. Could any lowland living possibly fill that gap? It seemed doubtful that it could, yet it did. Even before I properly saw this land I was hooked.

We came down the hill into the village unseeing. November, it was, with grey fog and empty trees dripping. There were no views, for they'd been swallowed by that cold, aching fog. Yet through the dank, blind mist one could sense, not see, a big panorama of space, and before even we reached the gate that would lead to work and a fresh beginning, we knew, without any shadow of doubt, that this was where we belonged. Almost thirty years on we've not wanted to live anywhere else.

That view, which we couldn't see first time round, and the space it encompasses, has become cause for daily celebration, is part of the magic. But only part. Five minutes from where I sit and write these words I can be wandering a meadow that is buckling at this very moment. It is a restless earth, its configurations forever rearranging as subterranean forces ripple the surface, build hillocks, sink into hollows, spill waters over yesterday's dry slope, throw up rocks, build a wall round the base of an oak and invite ducks to nest among reeds where no reeds properly belong. Of course, one does not see or feel that movement. But go there, as I do, regularly enough, and you'll plot the changes that occur. Four centuries ago, over an eleven-day period, such movement was so profound that 'gentlemen' from a neighbouring parish came to watch and listen. This is what they found:

This great trench of ground, containing in length eighty perches, and in breadth twenty-eight, began, with the hedges thereon, to loose itself from the rest of the ground lying round about it, and to slide and shoot altogether southward, day and night . . . The ground of two water pits, the one having six feet depth of water, and the other twelve at the least, having several tufts of alders and ashes growing in their bottoms, with a great rock of stone underneath, were not only removed out of their places, and carried southward, but mounted aloft and became hills . . . and in the place from which they had been removed, other ground, which lay higher, had descended, and received the water on it.

And as the hillside rearranged itself so it made loud protest. The report gives evidence of this protest, for the gentlemen wrote of '. . . the cracking of the roots of trees, the breaking of boughs, the noise of its hedgewood breaking, the gaping of the ground, and the riving of the earth asunder . . .'

Four hundred years on and the wounds have healed. Or have they?

Greensand hills are thirsty hills. They soak the rains through a blotter of surface soil and filter it down to sunless reservoirs lined with a bed of clay. Springs spill out to allow some discharge, but in times of heavy rainfall these springs are insufficient to release unspoken pressure from below, and the meadow is forced to rise here and there in buckling motion. On the other hand, during periods of drought the water table runs low and movement is predictable, with forthcoming scoops and hollows signalled by tell-tale shadows. This unbidden work of reshaping continues, day in, day out. It is the miracle of Genesis reborn. It is the tireless evolution of this restless earth, and we its witnesses.

Aristotle was right when he said that in every natural phenomenon there is something wonderful. And another poet of another age claimed that we are born among wonders, and so surrounded by them that to whatever object the eye turns, that which we see is wonderful – if only we will take time to examine it. If only we know *how* to see.

But cross this meadow and over a stream, then up another meadow to a stile and a flight of a hundred and thirty-odd steps through a private garden, intoxicating in spring with fragrance that attacks you on the way up, and on to a lane that seems to hang from the hill like a terrace ready to fall. The poet Richard Church once wrote of this lane that it cut through soil so rich and deep that everything, wild or cultivated by man, rioted so luxuriously that he was reminded of a grove in Sicily. But gaze through that luxurious growth and a light comes flooding as pure as the light of Tuscany. It is the very light of the South.

An old timbered farm and a clutch of white-tipped oasts hang from the slope and greedily soak that light, slightly protected from the battering of westerlies by a projecting nose of hillside riddled with badger setts. Above the farm more steps climb steeply on to the uppermost lip of the hill. A path entices forward. Another breaks off to the right and meanders through a natural avenue of birch, beech, ash, oak and hazel – and in late April or early May a dense waft of smoky blue carpets every square foot of ground. Bluebells, everywhere.

The footpath twists, rises and comes to a brief opening – and the slope falls away upon the topmost leaves of sunken trees, and reveals an outlook to the west that will catch your breath with delight. Can this possibly be the overcrowded south-east of England, with Hyde Park Corner not twenty-five miles away?

Everything near at hand is green; a dozen shades of green, many of which change and adapt with the seasons. Trees, hills, meadows, woodland shaws, spinneys and near-black woods in bold formation fold one upon another out to far distant horizons where green turns to blue and earth is lost against the sky; a seamless horizon too far to count. Out there, towards the sunset, our Greensand Ridge curves gently and appears to slide into the Weald, rather than form a wall to it. Those hills are among the highest patches of land for many a broad county. Yet in distance they're almost flat, and it's only because we've walked them, puffed and panted over them, that we know their true dimensions.

Our hill is a lofty eminence, too. Well, lofty for the southern counties. And it's special. Here on this west-facing fringe there's a stone seat erected in memory of her mother by Octavia Hill, one of the three co-founders of the National Trust, who built a cottage nearby and who lies in the shadow of the Greensand Ridge beneath a knobbly yew in the churchyard a mile away.

Although her life's work was concerned with housing reform, it is my firm belief that Octavia Hill's major achievement, and her most important legacy, is not in her tireless struggle to improve the quality of life for London's slum dwellers, nor in the subsequent and much-lauded protection of historic buildings via the National Trust, but in her far-sighted and deep commitment to countryside access, which manifested itself in the safeguarding of numerous tracts of priceless land. Mariners Hill is just one. She knew how precious such sites were – are still. She knew what it was to be denied a right to light and space, and once made an eloquent appeal on behalf of the disenfranchised poor in which she wrote of '. . . the need of quiet, the need of air, the need of exercise and, I believe, the sight of sky and of things growing [which] seem human needs, common to all men'. These things were so important to her and to those denied them that often she would refer to what she called in moments of inspiration, 'the healing gift of space'. 'Unless we have it,' she wrote, 'we cannot reach that sense of quiet in which the whispers of better things come gently.'

The whispers of better things come gently. And come gently they do here on Mariners Hill. I've stood here, sat here, lain here many hundreds of times, in all seasons, in all weathers, at all times of day and night in the past three decades, and heard the whispers of better things come gently. On an early morning chilled with dew or frost I've stood on the very crown of the hill and waited for sunrise. Me and the foxes. I've found myself marooned above the clouds – as wonderfully profound as on any mountain summit – all the valley below swallowed by the vapour and only an archipelago of treetops making tiny islands in that sea. Towards dusk I've bullied others to Miss Hill's seat and drawn the glory of sunset around us, then walked in Indian file across the brow and beneath a frieze of feathers as pheasants roosted on branches overhead before returning in black night to the village below.

By day you'd be hard put to believe in the populated valley below. But by night the great expanse of the Weald sparkles like the buttons on a Pearly King's jacket as one light after another betrays the existence of a farm, a cottage, a clustered hamlet or village otherwise hidden by the riotous foliage that is green, green Kent.

How stealthily did Octavia Hill work to safeguard this vulnerable site, this belvedere in the sky! Little by little she made her purchases, rarely with anything but subterfuge in order to keep her identity unknown, until there was just the very summit and the eastern slope left. In a letter that clearly reveals her passion, she wrote, 'If we do get this additional slope, all our view to the East will be unimpeded land and sky giving delicious sense of space. Imagine the joy of that hilltop with all its view and air . . . leave it free for those that love it, and will find joy and peace there for years to come.' On the day before she died she was handed a cheque that finally secured all of Mariners Hill in the name of the National Trust – but for all people, for all time.

Mariners is just one of many such hills and viewpoints for which we owe a debt of gratitude to the memory of this formidable Victorian lady, and since she knew this Greensand Country so intimately, and fought with such vigour to ensure access to it, it comes as no great surprise to find that all along the ridge the familiar oak-leaf and acorn symbol of the Trust appears on posts to mark land in care and where one may almost guarantee a discovery of that healing gift of space. The next hill to the east of Mariners, for example, is Toy's Hill – 'the first beautiful site in England dedicated as a memorial' – then comes Ide Hill, 'the breezy hill, wide view, woodland glades, tiny spring, all yours and mine and every citizen's for all time to come'. To stroll from one to the other provides a morning's exercise as rewarding as any I know.

Back of Mariners, a web of footpaths criss-crosses the wooded common; other trails are there if you have eyes to see, but they're not the trails of modern-day ramblers, rather they belong to nocturnal creatures that belong here as surely as any of us seeking passage. Nights there have been that I've stood silent in the dark and listened to their passing, caught their musky smell and seen lights for eyes in the cold lunar beams; heard the soft pad and rustle of leaves and brushwood, the spooked scamper of the hunt, the muffled yelp and cry that followed. Primeval, perhaps, but part of nature's course.

A broader path cuts diagonally across the common and drops on cut clay steps to a lane. Across the tarmac and along a path enclosed by fences to left and right. Beyond that to the right a handsome vista appears through a deep cleft in the ridge. The eye is focused through that cleft, like a tunnel with only sky for a roof. And once again, out there lies the Weald, all open space tilted from the south where the long blue line of Ashdown Forest tells of distant Sussex. That is the horizon.

The mid-distance is woodland and meadow, while the near view is dominated by a gleam of water, neatly trimmed sward and a mansion seen side-on. This is Chartwell, home of Winston Churchill for forty-odd years.

The enclosed footpath rises uphill, the right-hand view growing, then shrinking as trees and shrubs crowd in and we come to another narrow lane. Over this a clear bridleway leads on; woods to the left, a row of beeches on the right, and through them the first glimpse of oast-houses on a slope of green backed by storm-damaged woodland. When we come to the hamlet of French Street, yet again we are forced to concede the magic of a rural idyll. And again we question the oft-imagined picture of this South as being an overcrowded, seething mass of humanity. Kent has more motorway miles than any other county yet here, on the lane in French Street, horses outnumber cars, sheep outnumber horses in the meadows, meadows outnumber roads. And peace prevails.

We could head to the right here for a direct approach to Toy's Hill. I prefer a different way. For that we bear left to pass a bow-walled cottage as white as snow and as unreal in thatched perfection as a scene from Arthur Rackham, then cut off to the right on a plunging slope treacherous after rain or in winter ice when crampons would hardly seem out of place. A brook slides along the base of the hill, and over this the opposite slope is, fortunately, not quite as severe as that we've just descended. At the head of the first meadow a permitted footpath, offered in the name of the National Trust, teases to the right along a farm track initially, while the 'old way' continues up and onward to Pipers Green and the north side of Toy's Hill; inviting enough, 'tis true, but lacking the intensity of space and contrast offered by our chosen way. So off to the right to pass below a charming brick cottage and a pair of square-cut oasts hidden from the world by sheep-grazed acres topped by yet more woodland. The old cowshed here has been converted to dormitory accommodation for the use of conservation volunteers at work on Trust property. Snug it is, tucked in a little hollow without the views but sheltered from the wind and weather. For views, and these are views to remember, one need only walk but a few yards and gaze north, and there this lovely V-shaped valley draws the eye not to the Weald, as we've grown accustomed, but beyond the hint of the Holmesdale valley which cuts across our line of vision, to the stark wall of the North Downs. At the foot of those Downs, unseen, thank heaven, runs the M25. Beyond those Downs, likewise unseen, thank heaven, lies suburbia and the horror of London.

And what is our gift? Standing here in a gentle meadow fluffed with sheep whose wool snags the fences, with birdsong behind and the luxury of nature's benevolence all around, we know again the healing gift of space.

How we've needed that healing!

In the early hours of 16 October 1987 hurricane-force winds thrashed this southern countryside. As the pale light of day stole over the Greensand Ridge the landscape had changed. At Toy's Hill literally hundreds of acres of glorious beechwood had turned into a battleground, a scarred wasteland of twisted timber, where thousands of huge, prostrate trees lay scattered as if some gigantic game of pick-a-stick had taken place. I went there a couple of days later and wept for the glory that once was. There I found that sixty-foot trees, weighing Lord-knows-how-many tons, had been uprooted and were now supported by the shattered spikes of their one-time neighbours. Those once mighty beeches had been plucked from the ground like outsize leeks and tossed in the wind, their wrenched-off root systems now surrounded by vast discs of earth leaving pits that filled with water. The smell of decay was in the air. There was no birdsong. Deer stood wide-eyed and bewildered. Nature had fallen silent. In grief.

But the world of nature adapts to such crises. Better the wind that causes such nightmare scenes than the malevolent hand of man. And if we banish sentimentality, wipe away the tears, give time and distance and then look anew, we can find reason for hope. The evolution of the seasons helps make amends, and if we work *with* nature, rather than *apart* from it, in partnership, as it were, then the healing process is both speedier and more complete. The longed-for recovery of Toy's Hill continues at a steady pace. New trees arise from that awful devastation and a canopy of foliage ascends year by year towards the sun.

A broad path climbs on to Toy's Hill and weaves its way across the dome where still stand weather-bleached remains of fossil trees among self-sown birch and pine, the thousands of newly planted hardwoods, and dense banks of rhododendron that appear extravagant in June. Long vistas gained in the aftermath of the Great Storm are now slowly disappearing once more. In summer, that is. But in leafless winter the Weald lies revealed in splendour.

For a better, clearer view of the Weald one should break away from the wooden crown of Toy's Hill and amble down the slope a little to the few houses and cottages that represent the village itself. Most of these line a narrow lane cut, like that below Mariners Hill, as a terraced ledge facing south. A short way along this lane there stands a capped well-head: one-time gift to the villagers from Octavia Hill, who once owned the cottage that stands above and behind it. Before she sank this well in 1898 local women were forced to descend to Puddledock where they could fill their buckets from a spring, then return with their heavy loads up the rutted track to their homes on the hillside. But it is said that on the occasions when Miss Hill was away, some of the women resumed their journeys of old, for they found winding their buckets from the well almost as exhausting as the labour of carrying water uphill.

This well-head and the patch of land around it now belong to the National Trust.

With evident satisfaction Octavia wrote: 'Seats have been placed where villagers and visitors can sit and watch the lights and shadows over the whole magnificent sweep of country of which the terrace commands a view.' It is a vast panorama, complete in itself, full of enticement and rich in uncluttered perfection.

There is sanity in a wide view, and wide views are plentiful in Greensand Country. But sometimes we allow the whole to blind us to the individual wonders of the countryside where minute prints tell of vole and dormouse, where half-nibbled shells reveal evidence of a macro world every bit as magical as the overall scene witnessed from six feet above the winding trail. Could we but shed our veil of adult sophistication and reprise the sense of wonder that is the treasury of childhood, we would fill our days with joy.

On the east side of Toy's Hill the woods are named in honour of Octavia Hill. Many of the storm-flattened trees and the stark gesticulating fingers of former trees, have been left as a reminder of nature's power and fury – and as a heavyweight habitat for innumerable insects and the birds and creatures that feed on them. The sound of drilling often accompanies our wandering down the path of the Greensand Way into the damp hollow that lies between Toy's and Ide Hill, and when the drilling stops sometimes we'll catch that swooping, undulating flight of a woodpecker, or the maniacal cackling laughter that gives it the countryman's name of the yaffle.

Over an innocent brook, one of numerous tributaries of the Medway, yet another open meadow draws us up a slope to a junction of paths. Again we walk in the footprints of Octavia Hill, for this too is Hill Country – land that she valued, and finally won for the infant Trust. Bear right over a stile and skirt a chaos of brambles with views back west to Toy's and south into space. The path slopes down to another stream easing from a spring, then up again, more steeply now beneath a bower of leaves towards the summit of Ide Hill. She had already bought a ragged parcel of land behind the church, with its graceful panorama and access from the hilltop village, but this approach was important too. Though not so pretty as the main site, she wanted this particular access so that every generation for all time may wander from one ridgetop hill to the other without fear of restraint. In August 1910 she wrote in a letter to a friend that she had driven to Toy's Hill '. . . and walked to Ide Hill to inspect possible future purchase. It was so lovely; the path by the stream promises well, and on the upper field the heath has really taken hold and was in flower; and the trees we planted begin to be a feature.'

That upper field blazes with gorse and broom round its fringe. To it come hundreds, maybe thousands, of space-starved townsfolk each year to breathe again the fresh air and gather the sunshine, to witness a far view and know without words 'the healing gift of space'.

This is Greensand Country, gift of Octavia Hill.

Welcome to your roots, you one-time nomad.

THE SPIRIT OF DARTMOOR
Richard Sale

'I solemnly swear to you, Sir, nothing will ever induce me to set foot on Dartmoor again. If I chance to see it from the Hoe, Sir, I'll avert my eyes. How can people think to come here for pleasure – for pleasure, Sir! Only unwholesome-minded individuals can love Dartmoor.'

This quotation from the works of a Plymouth tailor and noted in Sabine Baring-Gould's *Book of Dartmoor* in 1900, is the most explicit, but by no means the only, reference to the moor's fearsome reputation as a place of featureless expanses, disorientating fogs and leg-devouring bogs. As early as the sixteenth century William Camden had referred to *squalida montana, Dartmoor*. Small wonder that when Sherlock Holmes met the Hound of the Baskervilles he did so on Dartmoor. Add a grim prison, and you would seem to have the perfect recipe for an area with no visitors and where any walkers you might meet were likely to have nails on their boots. On the inside, facing upwards.

At Two Bridges, the two main roads that cross Dartmoor (the B3212 and B3357) join to cross the West Dart river. The roads divide the moor into northern and southern sections: to the north is the higher land – tors and bogs, the famous walking country. To the south is a less frequented, more secret landscape.

The roads create eastern and western sections, too, though smaller. To the east is the tourist moor. By Haytor visitors can feed Dartmoor ponies (and themselves from a neatly positioned van that serves ice creams and hamburgers). There is an ancient tramway to follow, one that in the early nineteenth century hauled stone from quarries close to the tor. The quarries are a hazard to the young or foolish, but the tramway is much admired. Its rails were made of granite because cast-iron rails were prone to breaking. The local granite made good rails, and was a superb building stone – it was used on London Bridge – but transport costs killed the quarry, leaving the sites to the wind and the industrial archaeologist. Local stone was also used in the building of nearby Widecombe, Dartmoor's prettiest village, though the visitor has to avoid old Uncle Tom Cobley and all to see it.

Away from the tourist's moor, this eastern section of Dartmoor offers good walking. On Hamel Down lines of ancient boundary stones and even older cairns/barrows lead to Grimspound and Berry Pound. Grimspound is one of Britain's finest Bronze Age settlements with about two dozen hut circles, each around 15 yards in diameter, within a wall that, when complete, was probably 9 yards wide and 6 feet high.

Or go to Hayne Down to see Bowerman's Nose, one of the moor's most distinctive tors. Legend has it that entombed within it is a man who watched the cavorting of a coven of witches but was daft enough to laugh at their antics. In revenge the witches did not turn him into stone – that would have been too straightforward – but encased him in granite. He remains inside, fully conscious. When his wife and friends came to Hayne Down to look for him he could see them, but could not utter a sound. They came less often, and then not at all and he has been left to nurture his regrets down the centuries. Nearby Joy's Grave is real rather than legendary, and the sadder for being so. Kitty Joy was the daughter of a farm labourer who fell in love with the son of the landowner. He promised to marry her as part of his seduction, but after a long night of passion he threw her out saying he could never marry someone willing to have sex before marriage. The distraught Kitty went home and hanged herself. It would be good to report the young man's remorse, but he showed none and lived a long and (apparently) happy life. As a suicide Kitty was denied burial in consecrated ground and her body was interred at a junction of tracks to confuse her ghost as to its whereabouts and so prevent it haunting the area. For many years there was no headstone, but then curiosity overcome one local. Was Kitty's story just another myth? he asked, and dug up the grave site. Having proved the story he reburied her remains and added a stone. But truth and legend are never far removed on Dartmoor, and a posy of fresh flowers is regularly laid on the grave – by a ghostly hand, it is said.

A ghostly hand – huge and hairy – is said to haunt Postbridge. And, for good measure, a black dog is also said to haunt the hamlet, a favourite starting point for walkers exploring the northern section of the moor. There is little to see now to remind the visitor of Postbridge's prosperous past when tin was extracted locally, gunpowder was made, close to Powder Mills Farm, and a factory extracted starch from local-grown potatoes. The clapper bridge is one of Dartmoor's most attractive, its improbable height a tribute to the East Dart's winter floods. All of Dartmoor's clapper bridges have been dismantled by flood waters at least once during their history. All except one. It is said that the only time the Postbridge clapper was dismantled was when the locals used the slabs in an effort to stop a flock of ducks from swimming downriver!

The East Dart was high as I followed its eastern bank. That meant wet ground further on. A solo walker should think again, but Dartmoor attracts me because of its wild emptiness and there would be even fewer people today. The path is indefinite at times, but the river is the way. Where it bends sharp left, Lade Hill Brook comes in from the right. Up that valley a few hundred yards is the Beehive Hut, a well-known but poorly understood pile of stones. Some claim that it is very ancient, others that it is a tool hut used by last century's tinners.

The best route into the northern moor is to stay with the East Dart, letting it take you through Sandy Hole Pass – part natural, part man-made and certainly the best camp site for many miles – but the thrashing river persuaded me northwards on to higher ground. The compensation comes with the Grey Wethers stone circles. The moor was warmer, more hospitable when the Bronze Age folk erected the stones that form these two circles, but the fact that they now stand isolated merely adds to the mystery of why they were raised. A satisfying puzzle, made more enigmatic by the knowledge that at least one-third of the stones were re-erected in a general restoration in 1901 and that the site may have been 'renovated' by the Victorians. As any church-lover will tell you, Victorian restorers had trouble keeping their hands off anything, so who knows what the original stone spacing was? The circle figures in moorland legends, of course: it is said that any moor farmer's wife suspected of unfaithfulness would be taken to Cranmere Pool, washed in its cold, peaty waters and then brought here to kneel in front of a stone. If she was guilty it would fall on her. So if a dozen or so stones had fallen by 1901 does that make the Dartmoor wives a faithful or faithless breed?

I sat on Sittaford Tor and contemplated the way ahead. I'm told that the Tor is a murder site in an Agatha Christie book, but as I'm not a reader of her work I can't confirm it. Today, with the wind picking up and the grey clouds shutting down the sun it felt as though it should be. I cheered at the prospect of Quintin's Man, much visited in the days of my youth so we could all gaze in rapture at the legend 'Welcome to Quintin's Man, the Crutch of Dartmoor' painted on the hut wall. In those days the moor was beloved of Scout leaders who sent us on it at every opportunity, offering us tests that became sterner with each smiling return. I recall two of us on the northern moor spending three days with a meagre tent and sleeping bags, basic food and clothing that would make a tramp weep. We loved it and asked to go again. Today the Scout master would get the red card, perhaps even six months.

To the north, the Dartmoor range flagpole on Whitehorse Hill gives the way. Wildest Dartmoor is to the left now. In a light drizzle from a lead-shot sky, or in a clinging, soaking, deadening mist the line between land and sky becomes blurred. The effect can be disorientating, persuading the walker to go where experience tells him to avoid. In a curious, dream-like state, I once made for a patch of bright green, looking to rest, and found myself knee-deep in mire – featherbed – bog. Why anyone with a knowledge of the moor should be so stupid is still beyond me.

In the bogs to the west of Whitehorse Hill, the East Dart rises and runs south while just a few hundred yards to the north the Taw rises and heads northwards. But on Dartmoor the bogs are not confined to the valleys: ahead now, between Whitehorse and Hangingstone Hills, there is blanket bog. The red rocks of Dartmoor, formed beneath the sea of the late Devonian/early Carboniferous eras of geological time, were folded into the Cornubian mountains about 300 million years ago. Into the roots of these mountains poured the volcanic magma that, after the softer, overlying rock had eroded away, would be the granite bosses of the South West Peninsula – Dartmoor, Bodmin and Penwith Moors, and the Scilly Isles. Dartmoor granite comes in three forms, dependent mainly upon the rate of cooling of the magma. But whichever type it is, weathered granite produces a thin acidic soil, its poverty as a growing medium enhanced by its impermeability. In this waterlogged soil the few plants that do grow do not break down well when they die, their decay inhibited by lack of oxygen and the acidity that kills bacteria. The resulting semi-decayed peat matter forms a brown, muddy soup – peat, the basis of the Dartmoor bogs. The bogs support a unique flora – insectivorous sundew and the rare bog orchid. But it doesn't support walkers too well, so I took Whitehorse Pass, a 250-yard, or thereabouts, pass cut through the peat, offering a (reasonably) dry way through the worst of the blanket – upland – bog. Some of those passes are thought to have been cut by hand in Saxon times. Many of today's walkers would have their romantic notions shattered if they discovered that Whitehorse Pass was cut by bulldozer in 1963.

In spiteful but hardly savage rain, I followed the flank of Hangingstone Hill. If you come this way don't try the direct route to the top: the bog that way is a true definition of misery. Instead, contour around until you are below the top and then strike up. I guess there was once a white horse on Whitehorse Hill. There was certainly a hanging on Hangingstone Hill: a seventeenth-century mayor of Okehampton, Benjamin Gayer, who doubled as a sheep stealer, was brought here so that his gibbeted body could act as a local deterrent. In all but the best weather it would have been visible to almost no one.

I stopped on the hilltop and so did the rain. The clouds lifted a little, but resentfully as though to allow me a sight of the high Dartmoor hills would be to lose a personal duel.

Dartmoor's highest peak is High Willhays, the highest English peak south of Kinder Scout over three hundred miles to the north. The second part of the name is from the same Celtic root that makes Bodmin Moor's Brown Willy Cornwall's highest hill (from *bron ehwella* – Cornish for highest hill). It's difficult to take a peak called Brown Willy seriously, and Yes Tor does the same thing for High Willhays. It is a much better peak, distinct and distinctive. If it wasn't for the Ordnance Survey's insistence that High Willhays is a few feet higher you might ignore it on your way to Yes Tor.

I dropped down off Hangingstone Hill, heading westwards through the bogland close to Taw Head towards Cranmere Pool. The military road from the Okehampton Camp allows drivers not intimidated by dubious fords and pot-holes to reach an observation post close to the Pool, making a journey to it much less epic than it was for early travellers. The first documented trip was in 1789 by John Andrews, a Devonian lawyer. By the early nineteenth century local men were guiding the intrepid to it. Then, in 1854, James Perrott, one of the local guides, built a cairn around a glass jar into which his clients could drop a visiting card. He added a visitor's book and in 1937 a letter-box was erected: drop your self-addressed postcard into the box and take out the last visitor's card, posting it back to him. After the letter-box was installed, the idea spread. Today there are rumoured to be a thousand or more boxes on the moor. There may even be record cards for the stamps and societies for the stampers, but I don't know – it's a little too close to trainspotting for my interest.

Benjamin Gayer's spirit, condemned to hell after his earthly body had struggled its last on Hangingstone Hill, was set the task of emptying Cranmere Pool with a sieve, a task his personal demons reckoned would involve an eternity of misery. Visitors on a dry day might think Gayer had succeeded. A hundred years ago a storm or, more likely, a deliberate human hand breached the peat walls enclosing the pool. Had he been punished enough? Now, only after wet weather is there a real pool. Then it is no problem to find – it's everywhere, even in your boots.

Just like today. I headed westwards to the memorial to Frank Philpotts, who cut many of the moor's peat passes. The memorial marks the northern end of the Black Ridge Pass, which leads to the valley of the Black Ridge Brook. The valley crossing is fun for water lovers and another peat pass can then be used to reach Cut Combe Water. The object is to get to Fur Tor. Many will point out that Black Hill/Cut Hill is a more sensible route. And so it is. But where's the adventure in that?

Fur Tor is the 'Vur Tor', the far tor in the local dialect. It is aptly named, being the point of inaccessibility of the northern moor. In Dartmoor legend the tor is the home of the little people: only thirty years ago a walker claimed to have seen a pixie sitting on the top. Earth Magic believers claim that the tor is a source of natural energy. Certainly it can be an eerie place if you are alone in moody weather: the tall rocks with their odd slots and niches.

On the southern side of Cut Hill the North-west Passage peat pass allows a return to the East Dart near Sandy Hole Pass. In drier weather you can cross here, but today the river was fast and dirty, the waterfall sleek and noisy. I drifted down Drift Lane. At its end the throng at the National Park building welcomed me back from the land of myth and legend.

The western section of the moor, the triangle between the B3212, B3357 and the western moorland edge includes the Merrivale menhirs, one of Dartmoor's most impressive megalithic sites, and the Princetown prison, its most imposing building. The Merrivale site consists of two stone rows, a stone circle, several cairns and standing stones. The two rows are not parallel, but it has been calculated that if they were erected about two hundred years apart then they could each have pointed to the rising point of the Pleiades in May, the time of reaping. The Greeks used the setting of the Pleiades in November to time their planting; Australia's Aborigines believed the Pleiades brought the heat of summer and were more important than the sun. But did an agrarian folk really need to observe a star group to know when their harvest was ripe? That is just one of a number of questions about this most enigmatic site. What rituals were performed at the rows and circles? Who was buried in the *kistvaens* (small stone boxes)? The real mystery, perhaps, is the apparent sophistication of what we call primitive people, the extreme complexity of a few simple stones.

There is little mystery about the prison. It was built in the early years of the nineteenth century to provide work for the folk of Princetown, an enthusiastically constructed but badly conceived town build by Thomas Tyrwhitt, an Essex man. Tyrwhitt was a student friend of the Prince of Wales, was appointed Auditor of the Duchy of Cornwall in 1786 and called his new town after his benefactor. The prison's position was handy for the transfer of French and American prisoners-of-war from the rotting prison hulks at Plymouth, though by all accounts the conditions in the new building, opened in 1809, were little better. Tyrwhitt, meanwhile, had transferred his enthusiasm for making money out of Dartmoor to the construction of a railway from his quarries on King's Tor, just south of Merrivale, to Plymouth. He wanted to export stone and import lime to sweeten Dartmoor's acid soil, turning the moor into a pastoral paradise. So late was his railway in opening that he lost the contract for supplying building stone for London Bridge: some of the corbels finished for the bridge still lie beside the old track. He didn't manage to sweeten the moor either, leaving it, apart from the quarry scars, as wondrously wild as he found it.

On a crisp early spring day, the air clear and filled with cool sunlight, Mike and I left the parking place close to the tree-fenced Scout hut to explore the southern moor. We soon abandoned the deep track for Drizzle Combe and its standing stones. The combe seems aptly named: each time I had come – but to be fair that wasn't so many – it had rained, that fine, clinging rain that explores every crevice of your rainwear and eventually winkles out all the dryness. The tallest of the menhirs at Drizzle Combe, a stone more than nine feet high, is the tallest on Dartmoor. It stands at the end of a stone row, the whole combe filled with cairns and the remains of early settlements, yet more evidence of the moor's spiritual history.

We followed the river Plym north-eastwards, crossing at Plym steps where in all but the wettest weather the river is a quick hop or two wide. We crossed Langcombe Brook, too, following its southern bank so we could peer into Deadman's Bottom, much to Mike's amusement. Then a detour to Grim's Grave, just for fun, before climbing Langcombe Hill, a shallow peak with a high plateau-like top that almost obscures the view. We edged south to admire Stall Moor. This southernmost section of the moor is exquisite, bleakly magnificent uplands cut deep by gentle, sculpted valleys. Mike found new-born lambs sheltering in a hollow, the ewe keener to show them off than to run. It was, he says, a tender moment, but one he hopes she will not be as keen to share with the Dartmoor foxes.

We descended over difficult ground to the stone circle at the end of the Erme stone row. The circle is known locally as The Dancers from a legend that the stones are young girls petrified for dancing on the Sabbath, a tale that recalls the similar legend behind the name of The Hurlers on nearby Bodmin Moor. The Dartmoor stones have long held a special place in the minds of the moor folk. Beside the river Erme, tinners worked ore from the ground over many years. But they would never touch the stones, fearing the wrath of the spirits of those who raised them, or of the gods they raised them to. If their work required a stone to be moved, the tinners would carefully restore it.

Though much less spectacular than the huge rows of Carnac, or Avebury's avenue, the Erme row is the longest in Europe, perhaps in the world, stretching almost two miles from The Dancers to Green Hill. The stones are not worked and were not selected for shape, as at Avebury. The row is not straight and cannot be seen in total from anywhere along its length: facts that seem to undermine the usual explanations for such rows. We walked along it. Surely three or four thousand years ago men were doing just the same. But which way? And why?

I would have turned with the Erme, heading for Erme Head where the old mine spoil heaps can be used as shelters when the cold Atlantic winds decide to explore the southern moor. But Mike was drawn north towards the row's end at Green Hill. Just to stand there and look and wonder.

So we changed plan and continued north, crossing the sodden flank of Naker's Hill. North now are the Foxtor Mires, a bogland that can drain the colour from the cheeks of the brave. At its edge – and that day, with its short daylight hours meant the Mires must wait – is Childe's Tomb, an ancient cross thought to stand above a Saxon burial. Dartmoor folklore tells of Ordulf, a Saxon leader who tried to escape death from exposure during a winter storm by killing his horse, slitting it open and crawling inside. It's a desperate remedy, warm but wet, so that if the storm continues death is even more certain. Ordulf died, his body was found days later and buried here in the *cild's* (leader's) grave. The site is sobering, more so as you look out across Foxtor and contemplate escaping from its clutches as a blizzard rages.

We headed west towards the dying sun, edging rising streams to reach Nun's Cross Farm and Seward's Cross. There is a story told of a traveller who sought shelter in an old, tumble-down house on the moor. The roof leaked like the proverbial sieve, the protection it offered being more in anticipation than in reality. The traveller, made more miserable by the dubious shelter, asked the farmer why he didn't mend it. 'You must be mad,' cried the farmer. 'Only an idiot would work on a roof on a day like this.' The traveller, now adding exasperation to cold, wet misery, persisted: why didn't the farmer mend the roof on a dry day? 'What?' the farmer cried, even louder.

'Waste good weather on a roof that isn't giving any trouble?' If Nun's Cross Farm was not the house in question it could have been.

Like Childe's Tomb, Seward's Cross is named for a Saxon lord, Earl Seward, who owned estates here before the Norman Conquest. The cross is first mentioned in 1240, long after Seward was just a memory, and is likely to have been erected as a guide for travellers on the moor. The Ordnance Survey, and others, insist on calling the route that the cross marks the Abbot's Way, but that is a modern name, first used two centuries after the last abbots had been evicted from the dissolved abbey at Buckfast and Whitchurch Priory, the conjectured route linking these two. But there was certainly a route, perhaps packhorses carrying wool, with the tinners using it later, and the cross is likely to have marked it, such 'Thank God' crosses being common on high passes or in remote areas.

I would like to have continued westwards to Down Tor and its stone row, but the day's early dawdlings meant that the sun was setting. Dartmoor eases time away from walkers like the best of pickpockets. There is so much to see, so much to do and, suddenly, the day is gone. So we took the easy way, the track to the Eylesbarrow tin mine, the last of the moor's mines to close, in 1852. It was a cruel place, the metal 'plating out' from ore-smoke drawn through a horizontal flue. Workers scraping the metal from the wall breathed an atmosphere heaving with metal dust and died as a result, their lungs and internal organs stuffed with heavy metals. It is hard to mourn the mine's passing, harder still not to sense the ghosts of the tinners walking down the track from it.

And, to the left, through dusk's gloom, the Drizzle Combe menhir stared up at us, as, for centuries, it had at other moorland travellers.

THIS OTHER EDEN

Doug Scott

Thanks to the quirks of climate, geology and human history, we still have in every corner of these wonderful isles natural places to find peace and quiet and to go out and beyond ourselves. There is one sure way to lift the spirits and that is to take a walk by a broad river through ancient woodland and to climb on a secluded crag facing the setting sun. Such a place is Armathwaite, which is, as it happens, only half an hour by bike from my home. I am not going to rave about this little bit of England in the hope that the reader will be tempted up here to see it all for himself – in fact, I hope you don't come! What you should do is to check out your own area first and you, too, might be pleasantly surprised as I was when I finally got round to checking out mine. So don't come here *en masse* to mess it up for me – and for you: you might find that the experience you sought has vanished because you are here with so many others. It isn't necessary to go half-way round the world as I keep doing, year after year, to find a little bit of how the planet always was: it is probably just a few miles round the corner or beyond the edge of town, and all the time you never knew it existed.

I had been living up here for five years before I took a walk down by the side of Croglin Water. It was good to take that Nunnery Walk down the hewn steps as William Wordsworth had, 'Now cleaving easy walks through crags and smoothing paths beset with danger . . .' and to come across a thirty-foot waterfall that burst upon my senses. It was all the better for being there suddenly, roaring down, collecting in a trembling pool of dark green water with a steep, mossy, sandstone crag rising up to a canopy of trees and that roaring, frothy, white force of water contrasting with every shade of green. The water left the pool, racing down through a narrow gorge, stopping in silent pools and tumbling on again eventually to join the level waters of the Eden. Walking downstream towards Armathwaite Crag there are giant oaks growing on the steep valley side, protected by the wind, drawn up straight in their search for light, and also fine beech, elder, Douglas fir and Scots pine and others I cannot label. There is such a variety of trees here that wildlife abounds on the forest floor. There are red squirrel, roe deer, fox and, apparently, mink. In spring, parts of it are a carpet of bluebells and in the autumn there are so many fungi, such as inkcap – so good to eat when fried in butter and milk – and the red *amanita muscaria*, brilliant against the fallen yellow birch leaves. There is so much more birdlife here than you usually see; far more than you ever see in a man-made planted forest, although there is some of that here, too, but it is well managed and not excessive.

The usual way to approach Armathwaite Crag is from the south, starting at Armathwaite Bridge, the way climbers have always gone but with some interruption in recent years. The present occupier of Armathwaite Place decided to erect an iron fence under the arch of the bridge to prevent people walking by the river along the grove of trees towards the crag. There was a ding-dong battle between the people's representatives and the landowner, but now that well over £100,000 has been paid over to the legal profession, things are back as they were but with access legally resumed down the broad path of stately beech, elder and oak. They were planted out in another century by the De Whelpdales, a wealthy Penrith family who built Armathwaite Place. However much I may resent restrictions on access to unspoilt and beautiful parts of Britain, there is no doubt in my mind that the landed gentry and landowners in general have, in the past, been good custodians of the land. There certainly hasn't been wholesale development and what buildings they have erected have usually blended in well with the countryside.

Just a few yards into the walk it is possible in winter to see through the trees across the river to Armathwaite Castle. This is a mainly twelfth-century pele tower, four storeys high rising up from the river. The building was extended during the nineteenth century and is now an apartment block – and not the most attractive of ancient monuments in this area. After walking along and out of the avenue of trees the river gets quite noisy where it tumbles down through a weir that was dynamited in the 1930s. It had been built on a volcanic intrusion, which cuts right across northern Britain from St Bees to the North Yorkshire Moors. On the opposite bank above the weir is the old corn mill, which gave cause for creating the weir to make a reservoir of water that could be led off through the mill. There is still quite a pool in the profile of the river here and otters play on its edge, and it has been reported that polecats have returned to this region. Just at the start of the north end of Armathwaite Crag stand the remains of an old boat-house. Since the blasting of the weir, it is high and dry above the water, but enough of it remains to demonstrate the skill and attention to detail the old architects and stonemasons put into their building work. Obviously, if a thing was worth doing in those days it was worth doing well to last beyond their own lifetime. The stonework weathers back into the land whence it came. There is dignity in the dying of ancient buildings.

Beyond the building the crag grows in height and drops almost straight into the water but there is an irregular way along the base if the river is not in flood. Even when it isn't, the sloping ledges – just a few inches above the water – are often slippery. There is an area of tangled root to cross and with head down, concentrating on that, it is easy to miss two faces standing proud of the sandstone where all the rock around is carved away. They are dead-pan round faces, inscrutable and mysterious, and there is also a carving of the salmon, which appears to have been done at a later date by a different craftsman. To the right of the salmon is a bay with some easy climbs, and beyond that another sandy-floored recess with crack lines for easy classic climbs on this Armathwaite sandstone. Here, on a smooth slab of rock, the members of the Mounsey family from Carlisle left their mark, inscribing a tribute to: 'The fishes' gentle life . . . other joys are but toys and to be lamented, only this a pleasure is fishing.' That was in 1855. There are three more faces, each to a buttress. Local legend has it that they were the work of a master stonemason, completed for his own enjoyment on days off from work. That may be so but they leave me wondering what levels of consciousness that stonemason could plumb and how he saw the human race. The inscription seems out of place but the faces don't, and they appear to have been done in an earlier period. They certainly have a presence and create a sense of wonder.

Beyond the faces the gangway is now more tricky, with water lapping right up to the edge of the rock, angled more steeply, and the river is quite deep here; deep enough for adventurous youths to leap off the crag into the Eden water. Having survived this stretch, a large, sandy bay is reached. On the left, facing upstream, is a huge, overhanging wall broken into blocks by long-gone quarrymen. The lower third is smudged with white; not the guano common on Eden Valley sandstone but chalk left by rock gymnasts, mainly from the Carlisle Climbing Club and other local climbers. Every Tuesday and Thursday evening these men and women exercise here, swinging around like their arboreal ancestors. To perform well on this wall you obviously have to watch your weight and climb regularly. A fair amount of natural ability and agility would not go amiss either. Even with all these attributes, a first-timer here may be easily discouraged, for the locals know the moves, and that is essential when so much of it is on the arms. These routes, as it says in Stu Wilson and Ron Kenyon's *North of England Guide*, 'put the arm in Armathwaite'.

There are two 3-star routes here; Time and Motion Man, and Exorcist. In the old guide they are deemed only 4c and 5c respectively but to me and most others of my limited ability 5b and 6a would have been more appropriate. However, they are both great routes: only thirty feet high but with a lot of character. The back of this bay is a pleasant Severe, given two stars, called Glenwillie Grooves. It is tempting to solo up this corner but the crux is a final move in the shape of an awkward layback crack. When the warm wet westerlies are bringing rain to the Lake District, here is one small corner of Cumbria that remains dry. The jutting, overhanging rock at the top of this part of the crag makes it popular for climbers but also for local people who come here to picnic, make fires, and camp right by the water's edge.

Further along, just beside the riverside path, there is a hollow at the foot of the crag. This is known as Hetherington's Bay. It is an excellent place to come and solo around, doing a girdle traverse all on the hands, swinging from ledge to ledge twelve feet above the ground. This is where the human spiders from Carlisle go backwards and forwards a dozen times a night and not many people venture above here. The Cally Crack starts off easy enough and looks quite tempting for those into hand-jam climbing, for there is a hanging block near the top that is split by a clean-cut crack, but it is deceptively thin and often damp. You have to be dynamic with a long reach to grab anything that is going to save you from a tumble backwards, as you negotiate this overhang. I have only been up here on a top rope, as with most of the harder routes at Armathwaite. That is within the traditions of the area; rather like the sandstone outcrops in Kent. Top roping is not unusual on the harder routes but, having said that, all the routes have been led and still are from time to time.

While Cally Crack seems solid enough, the majority of the cracks hereabouts cleave soft rock. One can imagine falling and the protection device exploding the rock all around it. It has been suggested that preplaced protection should be fixed in the form of bolts drilled into the rock but, fortunately, that has so far been considered an unnecessary option by the vast majority of climbers. As I say, all these routes are capable of being led by strong, competent leaders. It would really demean their achievements to reduce the climb for the sake of those lesser mortals such as myself. In fact, across the whole of Armathwaite Crag there is only one permanent point of protection and that is an old peg, which sits well one-third the way up Exorcist. To have bolts, brackets and chains strewn across this fine red desert sandstone would be an affront to the eye and would change the mellow character of the place completely. The mainly soft sandstone does not lend itself to this becoming a suitable place for frenetic sport climbing.

To the right of Hetherington's Bay there is a host of climbs but two of the best, and quite safe to lead at Very Severe, are Flasherman and Erection, both given a 3-star rating. They offer ninety feet of strenuous but always interesting and varied climbing. Here is a chance to sit at the top of the crag, bringing up your second, watching the river as mallard glide, kingfisher dart and the nervous dipper constantly dip from rocks in mid-stream. This is much more rewarding than belaying from the bottom with your nose pressed up against the rock down in the trees. Everyone else assumes that a climber climbs up, at least partly, to see what he or she cannot from below.

The final section of the crag is a multi-faceted series of walls and buttresses. The far end is a corner and long right wall. One reasonable route here – that is, if it's not sandy or green with lichen – is Barnacle Bill, which takes the corner up to the overhang. After some intricate face climbing it is possible to reach round the overhang to gain a continuation crack. This is climbed layback fashion, with some concern for the protection under the roof as the rubber of your rock shoes slides on the sandy slab. To the right of this is Andy's Slab. How anyone can climb this I haven't a clue. The Slab is bounded on the right by a very strenuous crack. It looks reasonable from below but is actually flared and thin, especially where it forks twelve feet up. This is Cod Piece: thirty-five feet of very hard climbing, especially if rainwater is still seeping through rock. It was first put up with the aid of two pegs but they have long since gone and it is now led free, but not by myself who can only ascend such difficulty with the comfort of a top rope.

With the explosion of interest in rock climbing throughout Britain – in fact, across the whole world now – a lot more climbers are coming to Armathwaite than ever before, and yet the crag is still in good shape. A few grooves have been cut into the rock towards the top of the crag where climbers have failed to fix long slings from the trees to prevent the rope producing flutings. A lot of care and imagination has to be put into arranging these belays to avoid the erosion that is so evident on sandstone crags elsewhere in Britain.

I would have written about another high sandstone crag upstream and on the opposite side to Armathwaite. Sadly, access has been prohibited by the occupiers of Armathwaite Place, who now own just about all the land on that side of the river right up to Lazonby Bridge. So for now, at least, to avoid trouble and possibly legal expenses we will have to be content with Armathwaite.

There is a good walk back through Coombs Wood alongside the Armathwaite Place field with its lone Sequoia and Highland cattle. The track leads to the Fox and Pheasant, a two-hundred-year-old coaching inn with a burning wood fire in the grate. Here you'll get Hesket Newmarket's very own Doris's ninetieth birthday ale and also a good welcome from Mo, the landlady.

Armathwaite, as the name implies, was just a thwaite – a clearing – in the great Inglewood Forest that stretched away west and up to the thinner soils of Blencathra and Skiddaw.

Nearly all our inheritance has gone for good but there are remnants to remind us – if we need reminding – of what was, for being in these woods has a familiar taste. How important these remnants of woodland are; a place to connect with great nature, to relax and feel the natural energy of the place and to go home a better man for that.

A Singular Place

Roger Smith

At the top of the ridge that leads up west of Coire an Lochain, the ground flattens out. West again is the severe slope leading down to the Lairig Ghru. North, the ground falls in a tumble of ridges and glens that gather into the course of the Allt Mor cascading down through the forest to Glenmore. South, the way I was heading, the ground rises gently towards Ben Macdui, around two miles distant and invisible from this point.

I stopped and sat on a rock, both to take a breather and to savour, as I had done so many times before, the magnificence of the scene looking across the headwalls of Coire an Lochain and Coire an-t Sneachda sweeping rockily up to the rim, which gathers them in and is itself a superlative walk. It was seven thirty a.m. on a perfect June morning. I had been walking for an hour and a half, and it was clear that this was going to be one of the great Cairngorm days.

As I attuned myself to my surroundings I became aware of something else: a very rare sensation. Not quite unique, for I have experienced it in these hills several times, but rare enough to warrant the sharpness of attention and stillness of mind I can summon, with some effort nowadays, as a result of several years' study of meditation when I was much younger. What I was listening to was silence. That is not a contradiction in terms. Silence can be heard in the same way as sounds: it is a very definite and particular aural experience, and in an increasingly cacophonous world can perhaps only be experienced in the fastness of the hills, and even then only through a fortuitous combination of circumstances.

There has to be no wind, a peculiar state of affairs in the Cairngorms of itself. There has to be no birdsong, nor sound of running water, nor other people within earshot. I had deliberately started very early to seek this quietness, but even then I was lucky in that the silence was undisturbed by even the most distant traffic or high-flying jet. It is a sensation that, despite years of wandering the hills and glens of Scotland and many other places besides, I have only experienced in the Cairngorms.

I sat, and let the silence fill and enrich me. Peace is a quality every one of us needs, more and more acutely as the world becomes ever more violent and noisy. I had been given a moment of peace, and was profoundly grateful. One more Cairngorm memory to be treasured; and the day gave a few more. On the summit of Ben Macdui I met a man who had slept there overnight. He was a keen glider pilot, and told me that the British altitude record for gliders, an astonishing 34,000 feet (10,700 m), had been set over the Cairngorms. Apparently the thermals here are as superlatively good as the landscape itself. I enjoyed gathering that odd piece of information atop Macdui at eight forty-five.

Later I traversed the shore of Loch Etchachan, a shining jewel in the sun. This is the highest sizeable sheet of water anywhere in Britain, and at nearly 3,000 feet it is frozen for a good half of the year. That day it was as tranquil and innocent as a boating pond in a city park. I walked down past the Shelter Stone to the west end of Loch Avon, and past the small sandy beach, which looks so odd there. I was back at my car at one thirty and heading home while most others were still in the middle of their hill day. I was very happy.

What it is that gives a particular place, or area, or group of hills, that sense of belonging every time you go there is something I have not yet discovered, and probably never will. It is the same with people. Apart from our own flesh and blood, we do not choose whom we love during our lives: in a real sense, they choose us. So it is with landscape, as far as I am concerned. It is a feeling of 'home', of caring and respect, of familiarity but never taking for granted. I have had this feeling for the Cairngorms since my first visit nearly thirty years ago. Even driving past on the A9, when time does not permit a proper visit, I am happy to look and recognize, in the same way as one might pass the house of a friend and smile, knowing he or she was inside.

And in that same way there is grieving, too, at some of the atrocities we have perpetrated on these hills. This is not the place for an examination of the issues surrounding ski development or forestry or the over-population of red deer. For almost all of the time I have known and walked in and tried to help care for the Cairngorms, committees and councils and working parties and conferences have sat and deliberated and produced reports enough to reach the top of Cairngorm itself. For all the words, precious little is done. There is some improvement in that more of the area is now in the hands of conservation bodies, but as a nation we fail our best landscapes lamentably, and arguably fail the Cairngorms most lamentably of all.

About fifteen years ago, during one of the battles over owner-ship and development, I walked with a friend from Linn of Dee past Derry Lodge and up on to Derry Cairngorm. Donald is a fierce Scottish nationalist and a man whose love of the hills is every bit as strong as my own. It was a clear February day and under their mantle of snow, the Cairngorms assumed a radiance that belied the normal ferocity of the winter climate. We came back down through Glen Luibeg. Suddenly Donald stopped, looked around at the glory of the hills and with a great sweep of his arm, declaimed, 'No man can own this!' I knew what he meant. It is ludicrous to think of 'owning' an area that has evolved over untold millennia and goes on evolving. All we should hope to do is act as its stewards and guardians. Sadly, even that small task seems to be beyond our reach.

What is this place that means so much to me, and to many others? Seen from the A9 at Aviemore, the aspect is of scalloped corries rising to what appears to be a vast plateau. This is a very simplified view of things, however. It is certainly the largest area of genuine upland in Britain and the only substantial area of land over 4,000 feet (1,215 m). It contains the next four highest summits (Ben Macdui, Cairn Toul, Braeriach and Cairn Gorm itself) after Ben Nevis, two high mountain passes (the Lairig Ghru and Lairig an Laoigh) of unparalleled gran-deur, and some of the finest rock architecture anywhere in Scotland. The plateau does exist, but it is riven with folds, indentations and faults that all go towards the unique character of the area.

Much of the rock is a beautiful pinkish granite that is quite unmistakable. Land me on a Cairngorm summit from a helicopter, blindfold, and as soon as the blindfold was taken off I could tell you immediately where I was. Oddly, the name 'Cairngorm' means *blue* mountains, and comes from a precious stone that was formerly discovered here in fair numbers. Very few are found today. Cairn Gorm is only the fourth highest summit of the range, yet it has lent its name to the whole. The more correct Gaelic name is Am Monadh Ruadh, the red mountains – more appropriate given the nature of the rock. This name distinguishes the group from Am Monadh Liath, the grey hills, to the west of Strathspey.

Many of the summits are merely the highest swelling of an extensive upland area. There are few genuine peaks in the way that Western Scotland has peaks. Some of the summits, such as Beinn Mheadhoin and especially Ben Avon in the eastern Cairngorms, are littered with huge warty tors of extruded rock. To bag your summit you must climb the tor, not always a straightforward business. The major glens run principally north–south and offer superlative scenery in places such as upper Glen Einich, ringed with frowning cliffs, and the middle reaches of Glen Feshie, a heart-stoppingly beautiful place.

On the northern side of the range is the Glen More Forest Park around Loch Morlich, busy in summer with watersports and with facilities such as a large campsite. Forest trails are laid out and you can visit a herd of reindeer, introduced to the area in the 1950s and doing very well – hardly surprising since the climate is not much different from that of northern Norway. Through this area runs the road leading up to the developed ski areas of Coire Cas and Coire na Ciste. Repeated and wearying battles have been fought over ski-development plans, the latest centring on a plan for a funicular railway reaching to 3,600 feet (1,100 m) on Cairn Gorm. The road ends at two car parks, both over two thousand feet up.

Away from this honeypot, the principle applies of the long walk in. To get into the hills from the south means starting at Linn of Dee, west of Braemar, or the road-end in Glen Feshie. The Linn of Dee start leads you either north up lovely Glen Derry or west down to White Bridge. All this is part of the vast Mar Lodge Estate, acquired in 1994 by the National Trust for Scotland and now the subject of radical and innovative management aimed at eliminating past errors such as bulldozed hill tracks, and regenerating the native Caledonian pine forest, which barely hangs on by a thread in the glens when it should cover a substantial proportion of the whole area.

To the east is a truly vast block of land with no roads. Through this area runs the river Avon, outflowing from Loch Avon via a notorious ford, which is not for the faint-hearted. 'Avon' means 'river', so we have the tautology of 'river river', but in this case it might derive from Ath-Fionn, relating to the great warrior of Celtic myth known more commonly as Fingal. Either way, the valley of the Avon is a most beautiful place. To its south bulk the hoary heads of Beinn a' Bhuird and Ben Avon, just a touch under four thousand feet and each of them mountains of contrast. Beinn a' Bhuird is 'table mountain' and it has, indeed, a long, flat summit area. To the west, gentle slopes fall away but to the east are stunning cliffs encircling high corries. Ben Avon also has fine cliffs around the Garbh (rough) Choire: and, of course, its fine rings of tors on the summit area, each presenting its own small but hugely enjoyable challenge to the scrambler.

You begin, I hope, to piece together a picture of an area of mountains whose summits are undramatic in themselves yet command highly dramatic vistas; an area of high lochs and lochans and sparkling burns running down through remnant pinewoods; an area of cliff-girt corries presenting many a challenge to the climber, summer and winter; an area of supreme beauty, wildness and grandeur irresistible to the lover of all that is finest in mountain landscapes.

It is an area that must be taken on its own terms, and you must discover over a lengthy period of time how those terms relate to you, your own frailties of either body or mind and your level of experience. A Cairngorm storm is a seriously frightening experience. The anemometer on the summit of Cairn Gorm regularly passes the 100 m.p.h. mark and goes far beyond it; at those speeds, especially in winter with the added severity of windchill, you are soon at the limits of human endurance for survival. Little wonder that these mountains have taken many lives.

The hills do not, as is often said, 'claim' lives. They simply are what they are, and we go there, or should, aware of what might happen and as prepared as we can be. In a white-out on one of the plateau areas, it may seem there is little you can do except pray for deliverance. I have walked past cairns in winter mist without seeing them, and at such times the danger of stepping over a cornice is all too real. I have basked on Macdui's summit on a February day when the sun had real warmth in it, and struggled off Bynack More in July in a heavy snow shower. I have, in fact, been snowed on every month except August in the Cairngorms. One wild August afternoon of whistling showers that mocked my attempts at self-protection I went up from Corrour Bothy on to Devil's Point (an English euphemism, incidentally: the true Gaelic name is Bod an Deamhain, but it seems that 'Devil's Penis' was not acceptable to

Victorian mapmakers). As I turned left at the top of Coire Odhar towards the summit I met another Cairngorms addict coming down. 'What's it like up there?' I asked. 'Snowing!' he replied. Great! I could complete my calendar year of Cairngorms snow! Unfortunately he was exaggerating; it was just very cold rain.

Through the heart of the range run the two great mountain passes, the Lairig Ghru and Lairig an Laoigh. The Ghru rises to 2,800 feet (855 m) and is a serious hill expedition despite being a 'pass'. Near its summit are the Pools of Dee and a little further south the Allt a' Gharbh-choire falls from the cliffs of Cairn Toul, atop which are the Wells of Dee. Together these waters run and swell as other tributaries are gathered in to form the river Dee, known for fine salmon and for the royal castle of Balmoral. 'Ghru' may be a corruption of 'Dhru' since the burn on the north side of the pass is the Allt Dhru or Druie. There used to be a laconic Scottish Rights of Way Society signpost in Rothiemurchus Forest, which said simply, 'Braemar by the Lairig Ghru. 25 miles. Unsuitable for bicycles.' The message seemed to be 'Off you go, good luck, but don't say we didn't warn you.' At Corrour Bothy, the route divides: you either head south to White Bridge and then east to Linn of Dee, or east to Derry Lodge, then south.

At Derry Lodge the Lairig an Laoigh joins. This is an equally arduous trek. From Glen More it swings round past Bynack Stables and rises to 2,400 feet (735 m) on the eastern flank of Bynack More, another hill crusted with tors, these called the Barns of Bynack but not forming part of the summit. The route then drops to the Fords of Avon, a notorious crossing point of the Avon over a mile east of its actual outflow from the loch of the same name. There is a small emergency shelter here. Once across the Fords the route passes the Dubh (dark)

Lochan and is joined by the path coming down Coire Etchachan to run down Glen Derry in very fine surroundings, with scatters of old 'granny' pines dotting the glen floor.

Note the name: Lairig an Laoigh, the Pass of the Cattle. This is an echo of past times when large herds of black cattle were driven from the Highlands to the markets of Falkirk and Crieff. Their routes seem almost unbelievable today: over the passes of Corrieyairack and Drumochter, or as here, through the Cairngorms to Braemar, then south along the route used by the A93 road today, rising again to well over 2,000 feet (610 m) at the Cairnwell. Walking down Glen Derry today, it is hard to imagine bellowing herds of cattle, with men, horses and dogs, all moving south. They generally covered about ten miles a day and rested at known 'stances', which were often supplied with a rudimentary inn. Dorothy Wordsworth memorably described the scene at a drovers' gathering at the Inveroran Inn, near Bridge of Orchy, in her diaries.

These hills are and always will be the essence of wildness, but they do have a long human history, and remains of shielings can be found in all the glens. Today we keep our habitation to the fringes, although there are several bothies, which are well used by walkers and climbers either as overnight stops on the way through or as expedition bases.

The wildlife includes, of course, the red deer, Britain's largest land mammal. There are many deer in the Cairngorms, and their numbers are being reduced steadily to give the pine forest a better chance: deer will eat as many young shoots as they can find. They have always been hunted, but shooting for sport with high-powered rifles is, in the Cairngorms scale of time, almost an innovation, starting only about a hundred and fifty years ago. There is less of it now, as the management of this area turns, painfully slowly, towards conservation and re-creation.

Of the birds, the true Cairngorms denizen must be the ptarmigan. Supremely well camouflaged winter and summer, its presence is often belied only by the harsh croaking belch that it makes. These beautiful birds, white in winter and a mottled grey-white in summer, live on the high tops as well as in the glens, and to hear them first, then catch sight of them if I am lucky, is part of a real Cairngorms day for me. In the early summer, ptarmigan chicks scatter at your approach, and more than once I have been led forward by the brave mother doing her 'broken wing' act, just a few yards ahead of me, to protect her chicks. How I wished that I could reassure her that I meant no harm. I have crossed these hills north to south, east to west and vice versa, and explored them many times, yet there are still untold numbers of corries, lochans, side glens and subsidiary summits that I have never visited and probably never shall. It is not always the highest hills that give the most memorable days. Sgurr Mor is a relatively easy walk from Linn of Dee, yet this Corbett gives fantastic value: because of its position it commands a truly amazing view looking north into the very heart of the Cairngorms and taking in Devil's Point, Macdui, Derry Cairngorm and much more.

The Feshie hills are also favourites of mine. To walk up from Achlean at the Feshie road-end by the gentle path to Carn Ban Mor gives no hint whatever of the glories ahead. Turn north and things start happening. The back of Braeriach comes into view, corried and carved. The slope dips and rises and ahead is Sgorr Gaoith, the Peak of the Wind. Its summit rocks are on the very edge of a stupendously steep drop into Glen Einich, with Loch Einich a dark shadow far below. The edge continues over the Sgoran Dubhs, Mor and Beag, and if you want you can just keep going right down past Clach Mhich Callein, the Argyll Stone – but your car will be far away by then.

Feshie also gives the drama of Coire Garbhlach, a fearsome ravine. Heading east from its top leads you across the Moine Mhor, the great moss, no place to be in mist or snow unless you know what you are about. Up here at nearly three thousand feet is Loch nan Stuirteag, Loch of the Black-headed Gulls, and yes, you do find them there. To hear gulls crying and ptarmigan croaking at the same time is an oddly unnerving experience.

As I get older, I shall find it harder to penetrate the heart of this range, the true Cairngorms, where there is no sign of man except the paths our boots have made. No matter. I shall still enjoy exploring the lower hills and outer parts of the area, and looking up at the great mass that has given me so much true refreshment of the spirit over so many years. I can look at my efforts to capture the Cairngorms on film: moderately successful as far as the shapes and colours are concerned, wholly unsuccessful where the land's soul lies. And I can look, as I am doing now, at maps, and trace past explorations, and dream of plans that will never be fulfilled.

Mountain names fascinate me, and I try to learn the meaning of as many of them as I can. The Cairngorms are full of wonderfully evocative Gaelic topographical names: Coire an-t Sneachda (Corrie of the Snows), Sgor Gaoith (Peak of the Wind), Leabaidh an Daimh Buidhe (Bed of the Yellow Stag), and, of course, that Devil's appendage ... But I think my favourite is an insignificant little hollow on the north-east flank of Derry Cairngorm, overlooking that great crossroads where Glens Luibeg and Derry meet. Many thousands of walkers pass through it each year, but probably few know that above them is little Coire Craobh an Oir – the Corrie of the Wood of Gold. I can only think this was named by someone who knew the soul of the area and loved it well. When the sun catches the old pines at a certain angle, they do glow with the burnished sheen of old gold. To walk through those pines, the Wood of Gold, and up beyond them into the high wild Cairngorm hills has been for me a joy beyond price. Perhaps, one day, someone who knew me well will take my ashes and scatter them in the Corrie of the Wood of Gold, so that a little part of me stays in these hills for ever. I could ask for no more.

THE KINDER CAPER

Roly Smith

I can never hear Ralph Vaughan Williams's *Fantasia on a Theme by Thomas Tallis* without thinking about Kinder Scout. It's an association of ideas, of course, because it instantly takes me back to the days in the mid-1970s when I was an information assistant doing weekend duties at the Fieldhead Visitor Centre of the Peak National Park at Edale. Our designer had just completed an audio-visual slide-tape programme, which brilliantly expressed her personal love affair with the mountain, and that was the music she had chosen to go with it. It fitted the programme and the mountain well, perfectly expressing the sombre majesty of the highest point in the Peak.

The audio-visual theatre adjoined the information desk, but

we'd made the mistake of allowing visitors to start the programme for themselves by pressing a button. It lasted for about
twenty-five minutes and, of course, it was played constantly
as people watched it, or idly pressed the button, got bored,
and walked out. So when those quietly ecstatic, rhapsodic
passages start ringing in my ears, I'm instantly transported to
the tors and moors and the cloughs and groughs of Kinder
Scout, and I suspect I always will be.

Like many walkers before me and I'm certain many more since,
I'll never forget my first encounter with Kinder Scout. It was
the early seventies, and I had escaped the choking confines of
strike-torn Coventry with Stollsie, a fellow journalist, for a
day's walking in the Peak. I remember the paper's somewhat
supercilious drama critic asking us, in all innocence, who was
this more benevolent member of the popular boys' youth
movement we were meeting in Derbyshire. At the time,
we didn't know much more about Kinder than him other than
the name's correct pronunciation. Neither of us had been there
before, but I'd read up what looked like an interesting route
delineated by Walter Poucher in that scratchy white pen, which
had been my introduction to the hills long before I could read
a map.

We set off from the neat National Trust hamlet of Barber
Booth and into the gradually narrowing ravine of Crowden
Brook. There was, and still is, a feeling of a Highland glen in
the grand interlocking spurs of this approach to Kinder, and
it remains one of my favourite approaches to the hill. Graceful
rowans wept over tumbling waterfalls as the route soon gave
way to rough gritstone boulders and we walked up into the
silent heart of the hills, watched over by the looming buttresses
of Crowden Tower. Occasional light showers of rain did not

deter us, for there was the promise of sun to come. An exciting little scramble near the infamous Keyhole Rock eventually brought us breathlessly out on to the summit plateau.

What a sight greeted our unbelieving eyes! We had never seen anything remotely like *this* before, and we were simply not prepared for it. Simultaneously both Stollsie and I reflected that we could have been on the moon. A vast, rippling sea of peat hags and groughs stretched to the far horizon, with not a sign of vegetation or life of any kind. Paradoxically, we felt on top of the world but at the same time as if we were floundering at the bottom of an ocean of chocolate-coloured breakers of peat. Then, as the promised watery sun broke through the clouds, thin wisps of steam began to rise gently from the endless banks of peat. Kinder really *was*, as John Hillaby had described it, like a vast heap of dinosaur droppings.

The only sound to break the oppressive, primeval silence of this soggy wilderness was the now-familiar, 'go back, go back' warning cackle of a brace of red grouse, and the faint cheep of meadow pipits sounding, again as Hillaby had put it, 'like the last ticks of a clock that has almost run down'.

Overawed by the sheer wildness, we scrambled in and out of some groughs, trying to follow the streams of beer-brown water to the elusive summit. We knew it couldn't be far, but all we did was get more and more clarted-up with sticky, cloying peat. Eventually we gave up the unequal task and returned, older but immeasurably wiser, down Jacob's Ladder and back to Barber Booth.

Of course, I've been back many, many times since, and old Kinder has never let me down. It's always the same, yet somehow always different. Unfailingly big, moody and magnificent, Kinder Scout is truly more of a spirit than a mountain. It exercises such an overpowering, all-pervading influence on its surroundings that it is still repeatedly, but incorrectly, named on some modern maps as 'the Peak'. As Paddy Monkhouse, one of its finest chroniclers, pointed out, the Peak is a district, not a mountain. In any case, he added, anything less like the dictionary definition of a peak would be hard to find.

This indefinable spiritual presence, shared with other hills like Coniston Old Man and Ben Nevis, imparts for many people an air of mysticism to Kinder. At least one organization regards it as a sacred mountain. George King, founder and president of the Aetherius Society, chose Kinder as one of the world summits during his 'Operation Starlight' between 1958 and 1961. For his believers it is a potential storehouse for cosmic forces, and for those who know where to find it, there is a 'charged rock' inscribed with mysterious symbols among Cluther Rocks on the western side of the hill overlooking the watery eye of Kinder reservoir. This is apparently where the faithful will gather on the Day of Judgement to be transported to a different, but surely no more beautiful, world.

Just visible from Cluther Rocks is the fabled Mermaid's Pool, a dark and brooding tarn that promises immortality to anyone who encounters the fish-tailed beauty on Easter Eve. And before you scoff at the legend, let me tell you the story of Aaron Ashton of nearby Hayfield, who was a regular visitor to the pool on the appointed day and who lived to the patriarchal age of 104, dying in 1834.

In physical terms, Kinder Scout is a fifteen-square-mile plateau of peat bogs, hags and groughs ringed by a sparkling diadem of gritstone tors that would not have seemed out of place in the studio of Henry Moore. In truth, the only places in which Kinder remotely resembles Dr Johnson's definition of a sharply pointed hill is when it sends out one of its shapely courtiers, like Fairbrook Naze, as seen from the Snake Road, or Ringing Roger, from Golden Clough, to tempt those who seek an audience with the mucky monarch.

Stories of first-time visitors who, like Stollsie and me all those years ago, seriously underestimate the modest 2,088 ft (636 m) summit of Kinder are legion. You'll still hear them in the snug at the Old Nag's Head at Edale; tales of immaculately equipped Pennine Wayfarers setting out from the village bright and early, only to return bedraggled and completely disorientated the same evening, believing themselves to be at the next stop of Crowden-in-Longdendale. I've even seen a smartly dressed couple blithely setting off up the Pennine Way in Grindsbrook carrying a suitcase in each hand.

'Going far?' I asked incredulously.

'All the way,' they replied.

Many ramblers know Kinder only as the first gruelling stage of Tom Stephenson's Pennine Way. But how many know also that the hidden agenda for that great access campaigner's thirty-year fight to set up the granddad of long-distance footpaths was to open up the then-forbidden moorlands of Kinder and neighbouring Bleaklow? One of my most treasured memories of Kinder is when I walked with Tom, my still sadly missed mentor, up through Grindsbrook Meadows in the mid-seventies. It was just when the first horrors of so-called 'human erosion', in the form of a six-lane highway, were exercising the minds of countryside managers. Tom's views were revealing. Looking down at the path, he flashed that impish grin and said, 'It's no more ugly than the hags, groughs and screes of Kinder. It's as natural as a sheep track and, when all's said and done, I wanted the path to be used.' I often wonder what Tom would have thought of the flagged, almost urban pavement that now winds up through the meadows and across Kinder's shoulders, or the floated geotextile mats that take his 'long green trail' up England's backbone to Kirk Yetholm.

The other reason why Kinder occupies a unique place in rambling folklore is that it was the scene in 1932 of the fabled 'Battle of Kinder Scout' when five deliberate trespassers were imprisoned for riotous assembly. Their unwitting ringleader was Benny Rothman, an unemployed Manchester mechanic who had stood in at the last minute to address the crowd of around four hundred ramblers, who set out from Bowden Bridge quarry for a well-publicized mass trespass that bright April Sunday morning.

I first met Benny at the fiftieth anniversary celebrations of the trespass, when the bronze plaque that commemorates the event on the wall of the quarry was unveiled. Since then, I've been privileged to know him as a friend and come to appreciate the quiet dignity of this small man with such a large heart and unflinching principles. One spring day some years later I walked up William Clough, following the route of the trespassers, with Benny and his wife, Lily. Benny, then in his eighties but still going like a train, recalled the frustration felt by Manchester ramblers denied the freedom to walk on Kinder's then-forbidden slopes. 'Can you imagine,' he asked, 'what the young people from Manchester felt as they used the only two footpaths open to them skirting Kinder and looked up at the rugged rocks on the skyline, or saw the Downfall with its great plume of spray and heard all the stories of Kinder, and knowing that they weren't allowed to go there?' A red grouse clattered up from the heather barking its warning as we rounded Nab Brow for our first spectacular view of the Downfall across the Kinder reservoir. Benny greeted the grouse like an old friend. 'No,' he smiled in answer to its repeated request, 'I won't go back.'

We ate our sandwiches beneath a rowan in the lee of the

bank of William Clough, and Benny reminisced about how he'd been forced to write his spirited defence of the charges against him and the others in the pitch darkness of a Leicester gaol cell. And we reflected how that much-celebrated incident all those years ago had at first divided, then united the access movement, eventually becoming an acknowledged catalyst in the whole access to the countryside and national parks movement.

Yet Tom Stephenson would never accept this, claiming that although it was the most dramatic incident in the long-running campaign, it had contributed little to it. He often said that the best thing to come from the whole event was Ewan MacColl's celebrated walkers' anthem, 'The Manchester Rambler'. He could identify with the lyrics of the ballad,

> *I've sun-bathed on Kinder, been burned to a cinder*
> *And many more things I could tell*

which he acknowledged could only have been written by a fellow bog-trotting trespasser. His differences with Benny Rothman were not about the principle of free access, but simply about the methods by which it should be achieved.

For those generations of walkers, whom MacColl immortalized as 'ramblers from Manchester way', Kinder Scout was the nearest thing to a wilderness they could get for a sixpenny bus ride. But, of course, wilderness is as much a state of mind as a physical reality. I once took a party of visitors from various American national parks up Grindsbrook to show them the restoration work on the old Pennine Way. These veterans of the granite spires of Yosemite and Yellowstone were truly amazed at the wildness of the situation. As we rested just above the Golden Clough bridge and looked out across to the noble profile of Grindslow Knoll, one remarked: 'Hey, I thought you said you didn't have any wildernesses in your national parks?'

Despite its relatively modest altitude, Kinder should never be underestimated. And any Kinder aficionado who claims they have never been lost on the summit plateau is either a fool or a liar. I well remember the time I took an inexperienced neighbour up that favourite route via Crowden Brook on a claggy November day. We reached the summit plateau without incident and, heading for the Downfall in what was to prove both a physical and literal sense, I decided that in view of the conditions, we'd better stick to the well-worn perimeter track.

We hurried through the Woolpacks, that extraordinary collection of gritstone tors just west of Crowden Tower, feeling threatened by their menacing, almost bestial presence, which the mist had immeasurably magnified. They are also appropriately known as Whipsnade or the Mushroom Garden, but take their more correct ancient name from their resemblance to the bulbous, rounded bundles carried by the packhorse trains that used to take Derbyshire wool to the Cheshire Plain across Kinder, via routes like Jacob's Ladder and Jagger's Clough on the southern side of the hill. We passed the curious water-ringed Moat Stone and then the great anvil of Noe Stool, watching invisibly over the source of Edale's river in the valley below.

This was all too easy, I thought, and suggested that we cut across the western shoulder towards Kinder Low to reach the Downfall more quickly. My friend bowed to my years of bog-trotting experience, and we set off, staggering in and out of increasingly deep groughs, which reached Somme-like proportions.

After about half an hour of this, I was relieved to see a group of rocks looming out of the mist. They didn't look like the rocks around the Downfall, but they were strangely familiar.

Then I realized, to my acute embarrassment, that we were back at Noe Stool, having walked in a complete circle. That's when I was forced to swallow my pride and take the compass out of the rucksack. As I said, Kinder doesn't suffer fools gladly. In fact I have to admit that after nearly thirty years of tramping across Kinder, I have only once managed to find the summit – or 'Point 2088' as it's known to regulars. And then I had to be guided to it, on a similar day to the one described above, by Gordon Miller ('Gordon the Warden'), the Edale ranger for the Peak National Park for many years. And it was with Gordon and a group of Outdoor Writers' Guild colleagues that I met another of Kinder's great characters. You won't find the name of Gilbert the Grouse in any guidebooks, but he was well known to hundreds of ramblers who made his acquaintance on the tor-topped summit of Ringing Roger, which provides such a magnificent grandstand view of Grindsbrook and across Edale to Mam Tor, whose noble shaven head is encircled by its Iron Age necklace.

We'd been inspecting the work that Gordon and others had done on the badly eroded path up the Nab, and just as we left the rocky summit of Ringing Roger, we met a father and son coming towards us. 'Look out for a grouse just over there,' said Dad, pointing back the way they had come. 'He's almost tame.'

Now I'd heard stories of this legendary tame grouse before, told to colleagues at the Fieldhead Visitor Centre in the valley below. Sure enough, just by a National Trust exclosure fence beyond the summit, the plump, furry-footed gamebird appeared and strode boldly towards us.

Ignoring his staccato requests to retreat, we loitered and the photographers among us had a real field day as 'Gilbert', as we christened him, aggressively posed and pirouetted around us. Gordon explained that we were probably trespassing on his territory, and he wanted us off. Eventually, our curiosity satisfied, we moved off. But one of our number stopped to change a film and Gilbert attacked this isolated intruder, violently pecking at his legs.

The overgrazed peat moorlands of the Dark Peak are often referred to in guidebooks as inhospitable deserts for wildlife, but that late autumnal walk with Gordon disproved the theory. As we walked on above the shattered crags of Nether and Upper Tor, we were treated to the wonderful aerial view of a pair of sleek, black-winged ravens soaring effortlessly below us above Grindsbrook, their croaking calls echoing off the rocks. They have returned to Edale after an absence of thirty years, and were pairing up with a view to nesting. We also disturbed several mountain hares, just starting to turn into their winter-white, which burst from the heather at our feet as we cut across towards the northern edge, and Gordon showed us the strawberry-like leaves of the rare cloudberry thriving on top of the hags.

To know Kinder as well as Gordon, you must see it in all seasons. And when the Kinder plateau is white-over under a crisp blanket of winter snow, it is transformed into a semi-Arctic wilderness, living up to the latitude it shares with Siberia and Labrador. Walking across the plateau in these conditions is one of the great joys of the Peak. Then those ankle-sucking bogs between the hags and groughs, famously described by John Derry as 'the most featureless, disconsolate, bog-quaking, ink-oozing moor you ever saw', are frozen firm underfoot, and surprisingly fast times can be achieved in the crossing. This is when the classic Dark Peak marathons, like the Marsden–Edale, the Edale Skyline and the Four Inns, are traditionally accomplished and forty miles a day is possible to the real experts.

During the long hard winter of 1978, my photographer friend Mike Williams and I struggled through thigh-deep snow to witness the rare sight of Kinder Downfall frozen into a 100-foot-high curtain of sparkling ice. We had our snap in the translucent light of the cave which had been formed behind the scintillating ice chandeliers, and then watched spellbound as the climber who'd shared our picnic site took off front-pointing up the vertical ice with crampons and ice-axe.

We were suitably impressed but, mere walkers ourselves, declined to follow his example and set off down to inspect the frozen Mermaid's Pool on the small plateau above the skeletal trees of Peter Nook Wood. We didn't see old Aaron's mermaid, but we half expected to encounter Eskimo Nell because we came across the bizarre sight of an igloo, perfectly constructed from snowblocks cut from the frozen snowfield that surrounded the tarn.

Another even more bizarre winter excursion on Kinder involved OWG friends and colleagues John Cleare and Mark Richards on the occasion of the launch of our book on the Pennines. On a bleak late-February day (my fiftieth birthday), we started up from the Snake Inn on the famous Snake Path, opened a hundred years before by the Hayfield and Kinder Scout Ancient Footpaths Association. The waterfalls in Urchin Clough and Ashop Clough were frozen into tapering icicles and great tongues of snows licked in deep drifts on either side of the path as we ascended to the ruined shooting cabin near Upper Gate Clough. Here we celebrated the launch with a hip flask of warming whisky. Our two charming but somewhat bemused lady hosts from the West Country publishers were hardly prepared for the rigours of Kinder in winter, but we warmed them up further with an impromptu snowball fight on our way back to some steaming 'Snake and Pigmy' pies at the eponymous pub.

At the other extreme of the seasons, Kinder can sometimes resemble a desert more closely than anywhere else I know in Britain's hills. Sean Jennett, in his *Deserts of England* (1964), said of it: 'The surface of the plateau of Kinder Scout is a desert in the absolute sense, for nothing grows here, not a blade of grass, not a tuft of heather, not a cushion of bilberry, and, as far as I am aware, not even moss or lichen.' This is especially true of the area around Kinder Low, where even the peat has been eroded away by centuries of overgrazing, wind and rain to leave a Sahara-like expanse of receding peat banks and drifts of sparkling, silica-rich sand between the low, generally flat gritstone tors. It's humbling to pick up some of these grains of gritty sand and realize that, as they were washed down into the cloughs and streams that drain the plateau and out into the river estuaries which feed either the North or Irish Sea on this watershed of England, they will eventually be compressed again to form the rocks of tomorrow's world – and start the timeless process all over again.

Fire has also denuded Kinder of its peat blanket, whether started deliberately as part of a heather-management programme or accidentally by a thoughtlessly stubbed-out cigarette, or by lightning strike. Firefighting in high summer on these higher and dry moors is a thankless task. During the great drought of 1975, I was among the volunteers who helped to try to contain a moorland fire near the summit of Kinder Low, and I well remember the long treks under a merciless, scorching sun to fill our watertank backpacks from the nearest spring over half a mile away. No sooner did you think that you had put one section out than it would burst into obstinate smouldering life again. Once a fire takes hold in the peat –

which, after all, is a primitive form of coal – it can spread underground and burn for weeks, destroying a habitat that has taken thousands of years to form. The prominent 'bald patch' on the southern flanks of Kinder near Upper Moor is tangible evidence of a major uncontrolled fire in 1947.

In autumn one of the finest walks on Kinder goes up through the dusky pink heather banks of the Fair Brook from the Snake towards the northern edge of the plateau. Less frequented than the Edale side of the hill, the northern edges are every bit as fascinating. The emphatically named The Edge leads past the bold headland of Fairbrook Naze to Seal Edge, with its famous climbing crag known as the Chinese Wall and the prominent pugilistic Boxing Glove Stones among Seal Stones to Blackden Edge, culminating in Madwoman's Stones and Crookstone Knoll. But perhaps the finest heather moors of Kinder are the Leygatehead, Middle and Park Hall Moors north of Hayfield. I remember one golden September day sending up clouds of choking pink pollen as we marched down through the knee-deep heather across Middle Moor to the prominent white Chadwick's shooting cabin at the junction of the Snake Path.

Kinder Scout has been described as one of the most walked-on mountains in Britain, and it is certainly one of the most popular. For many people, including me, it was their first taste of a real wilderness, and will therefore always occupy a special place in our mountaineering memories.

Ernest Baker, author of the seminal *Moors, Crags and Caves of the High Peak*, was a pioneer turn-of-the-century trespasser on Kinder's bleak plateau, and he expressed its peculiar, eso-teric charms perfectly:

There is one characteristic of Kinder Scout which I think is quite unique in these islands. Sometimes when standing in the centre of the plateau, under favourable conditions, with the horizon falling on every side, and no ground within our vision higher than the curving lines of the moor immediately around us, one experiences that exhilarating sense of being actually on the roof of the world more vividly than when standing on the summit of a high peak.

It's that moment when the magic of Kinder Scout takes hold, and offers a sense of solitude and established stillness, older than the world.

Can anyone hear music?

A WHISPER IN THE WIND

Christopher Somerville

Make it a frozen evening in January, somewhere along the sea wall. Paint an enormous western sky smeared with green and silver, pierced by a tall flint church tower and the gaunt black sails of a windpump. To the east, a darkening marsh with the sea trickling out of iced-up creeks. Dot the mud-flats with curlew and redshank, delicately high-stepping; scatter some Vs of gabbling pink-footed geese across that huge sky. Place yourself mid-picture, well wrapped against the cold, binoculars round your neck, hands in pockets, moving with the heavy steps of someone who has been out walking all day. And behind the sea wall, not too far ahead, set the orange glow of a pub's windows, beckoning you in to a pint of Adnam's and some slow local chat. That's East Anglia.

Or again: put a blistering bank-holiday sun in the sky, a sparkle on the North Sea waves, and a coachful of hilarious teenagers on a promenade. String bunting between the lamp-posts, puff a cloud of straightforward smells across the fun-fair: diesel oil and candyfloss, burgers and onions, donkey dung, someone's beery breath, someone else's Amour de Nuit. Fill the air with battling sounds: three girls in fits of giggles, beatbox thump from the rides, gruff laddish shouts, dog barks and gull cries. That's East Anglia, too.

Or, on the other hand, draw a plough behind an immense yellow tractor, combing black Fenland peat into mile-long straight lines across the tracks of ripped-out hedges. The tri-angular sail of a boat in a hidden channel, cruising across a beetfield into an alder wood. A great black barn on a hill, its posts and braces showing the adze marks made by the carpenter eight hundred years ago. A medieval market-town centre of leaning half-timbered houses, ringed by vast acreages of charac-terless modern shopping malls . . .

To declare an interest: I love East Anglia. I lived there once, and still go back as often as I can. I've explored, mostly on foot, from the Essex marshes to the Norfolk coast, from innermost pastoral Suffolk to outermost corn-prairie Fenland. I've hunted it, but I can't say I've caught it. To grasp East Anglia, to have it nailed out flat and finished – that's a different matter. You know when you're there, all right – all of Suffolk and Norfolk, parts of Essex, bits of Cambridgeshire and maybe southern-most Lincolnshire. But where are the boundaries? The Thames estuary? Probably not. The Wash? Perhaps. The limestone uplands of Northamptonshire, the clay lowlands of Bed-fordshire?

East Anglia is a mirage. The harder you look, the more

dreamy and insubstantial its outlines become. It's more to do with a state of mind, a slowing down of the pulse and the clock; or with hints to the senses, a blend of waterbird cries and that dry, elliptical eastern way of speaking, the smell of sun-dried marshes and harvested corn, the taste of the beer and the look of the big translucent skies. Trying to cage East Anglia inside mere geography is like trying to catch a swallowtail butterfly. Better, really, to let it be.

'Essex, mate? Godawful place. All gold medallions and white stilettos, East End villains in big flashy houses . . .'

If that's your perception of Essex, a walk round the Dengie peninsula will change your mind for you. This blunt nose of land, as remote and self-contained as can be, is less than an hour's journey from London, but in an utterly different time-frame. Here, the clock means nothing: along the empty miles of sea wall you measure time by the slow in and out of the tide. Out at the tip of Dengie stands St Peter's-at-the-Wall. This is the oldest Saxon chapel still in use in Britain, unknown to all but a handful of worshippers, a wind-scoured survivor in the face of fifteen centuries of bitter North Sea weather blowing uninterrupted from Russia.

East Anglia and birdwatching are indivisible. The river Blackwater's broad muddy estuary sweeps the northern shore of Dengie, a winter haven and well-stocked larder of eel-grass for the dark-bellied Brents, tiny, tough geese that trek down to Essex from Siberia. A pack of them, passing overhead, sounds more like yelping hounds on a hot scent than seabirds. They feed round the fringes of a string of flat islands that runs north-east up the estuary – Northey, Osea and Mersea, lonely little slips of land linked to the shore by snaking causeways through the mud. There's a story and a half to each of those islands: Northey, where marauding Danes defeated the Saxons in AD 991 after a mutual hurling of insults across the Blackwater; Osea, a drying-out refuge for turn-of-the-century alcoholics; Mersea, where smuggling formed the island's economy and excisemen ventured at risk of their lives. I remember a dawn visit to Osea, watching the postman bicycling across the causeway, an ant-like figure against a huge red rising sun; and eating my first oyster on Mersea, forcing down the ball of fishy, slimy mucus to the amusement of a ring of grinning fishermen. .

There are other Essex islands, too, further north beyond the jangling sprawl of Clacton and the pursed-lips primness of Frinton, tucked behind the crumbling cliffs of the Naze in an inland tidal sea known as the Walton Backwaters. Arthur Ransome came cruising here in the years between the wars. He knew the islands well – Skipper's, Hedge-end and Horsey – and set his Swallows and Amazons adventure story *Secret Water* on Horsey. Joe Backhouse lives there today in the island's lone farmhouse, lord of three hundred acres of flat grass and sea wall, breeding Arab stallions and watching the terns and plovers, the fieldfares and godwits, the short-eared owls, and the seals that haul out to lie like fat old sunbathers on the mud.

When I first got to know the Backwaters, Joe's neighbour on Skipper's Island was Harry Hawkes, retired colonel of paratroops and honorary warden of Skipper's. Harry built his own house – it started out as the cabin of a monster houseboat he never quite got round to making. He made his own electricity, constructed a spindly jetty, built himself a raft from railway sleepers and three aircraft drop-tanks. 'I don't know what loneliness means,' he would say. 'I never get lonely. When I leave this island it'll be in a box, six foot three by eighteen inches.' So he did, a year or so ago; a man who loved birds, moths, unruly machines and his own good company.

Rural Essex – now there's a contradiction in terms, some would say. But get out beyond the not-quite-London fringe of Romford, Brentwood and Billericay, and north again past Chelmsford. Up there, in green and rolling landscape, you'll find a clutch of compact medieval towns packed with beautifully preserved half-timbered buildings four and five hundred years old, built by the wealth of wool merchants and manufacturers at a time when Essex – along with the rest of East Anglia – was surfing on the crest of an economic wave. Thaxted's silvery-beamed Guildhall and great church; Saffron Walden's narrow streets of tottering, bent old buildings; Coggeshall's gem of a Tudor woolmaster's house, the elaborately carved Paycocke's. All these were built on the woolly backs of the money-spinning East Anglian sheep. There are older and more evocative buildings than these, too: the cavernous Wheat and Barley Barns at Cressing Temple, and the even more venerable Grange Barn at Coggeshall. The timbers of Grange Barn's cathedral-like interior, built by the monks of Coggeshall Abbey, have been dated back to AD 1140 – probably the oldest barn in Europe.

In among the woods and fields of back-country Essex, fragments of ancient landscapes survive. Not far from Chelmsford the quiet countryside holds farms that still carry the names of their medieval yeoman owners – Jacklett's, Wickham's, Hobclerk's. Thrift Wood's gnarled hornbeams are coppiced and cared for by today's conservationists. Salt Lane remembers the packhorses bringing sea salt upcountry from Maldon. And the thick hedgerows along Charity Lane contain beech, oak, ash, elder, holly, hornbeam, blackthorn, hawthorn, a rich mosaic that may date back to Plantagenet times or even earlier.

Up beyond Colchester, Essex looks over at Suffolk across the valley of the river Stour. This was the landscape painted and painted again by John Constable, the mill-owner's son from East Bergholt. Dedham, with its tall church steeple rising from the meadows on the Essex bank of the Stour; East Bergholt, up on the Suffolk side, looking down to Flatford Mill; Willy Lott's cottage above the ford where Constable sited *The Haywain* – all are still here, astonishingly intact, hardly changed since the painter put them on to canvas and into the English psyche. The Stour slides gently by these lush green places, making its slow way down to meet the river Orwell between Harwich and Felixstowe, a river mouth whose undershot jaw marks the outermost corner of Essex. Across the tongue of water curves the downward fang of Landguard Point, the very lowest extremity of Suffolk.

Suffolk forms a great ragged circle at the heart of East Anglia. The county sits between the soft greenness of north Essex and the flinty clay uplands beyond the Norfolk border. The flat fens of Cambridgeshire hem it in on the west; shingle beaches and small muddy estuaries make up its gently bellying eastern coastline. In between, you'll find nothing, or everything, depending on how you look at things. Rural inland Suffolk is a lost and gone kind of place, bypassed by all major highways, a place of big old houses tucked away among woods, of mighty grain-baron agribusinesses and corporately owned estates next to fifty-acre family farms, of pheasant shooters and coarse fishermen. They don't take kindly here to townees who move in and lay down the law on hunting, shooting and fishing. Outsiders have been drifting in, nonetheless, to live the modest good life and conduct business with a computer in the spare bedroom and a fax machine on the sideboard.

I lived at Nayland in the Stour valley for six happy years. Essex began at Abell's Bridge on the southern edge of the village. But Nayland was Suffolk, no question about it; something to do with the un-Essexlike steep rise of Gravel Hill to the north, maybe, or the Barbours and green wellingtons that half the village wore. The other half, Naylanders since time out of mind, were said to be slow and difficult to know: 'Oh, they'll say hello when you've lived there thirty years.' Utter nonsense – a couple of games of darts in the White Hart, a 'Good morning' or two in the street, and we were right at home. The children swam and fished in the Stour, made dens in the Fenage at the bottom of our lane, went carol-singing at Christmas in the village square under the eaves of medieval houses. Our friends were gardeners, carpenters, City commuters, postwomen, artists, farm workers, writers, odd-jobmen, retired gentlefolk, publicans and sinners – a pretty fair cross-section of a contemporary Suffolk village community.

A mile away on the ridge stood the tall brick tower of St Mary's at Stoke-by-Nayland, a church painted at a distance by Constable. The great man had relations in the area, so he knew our two sister villages well. He painted the altarpiece of St James's in Nayland, but he missed the best view of Stoke-by-Nayland, the one we saw framed in a gateway every time we walked over to the Angel Inn at Stoke. The Angel . . . my favourite pub, among several, in all East Anglia, smelling of wood fires and wax polish, where the bar food is so good you don't bother with the restaurant, where I have talked more rubbish to more good friends than in any other pub.

Another mile brought you to Polstead, with its Red Barn Murder story known by every local schoolchild, and its circular pond to which my ten-year-old son bicycled with a friend one pitch-black night in a pelting rainstorm (unbeknown to his sleeping parents), returning home in the early hours with a carp and a mile-wide smile. Further on was Kersey, a tumble of miraculously preserved medieval houses hidden in a dip of ground, and Lavenham, beset by tourists, where each street seemed to vie with the next for the title of Quaintest, Oldest and Most Tottery. In the little Norman church at Wiston, just down the valley, a great red dragon ramped among saints in thirteenth-century wall paintings. Then there were those wonderful names of farms and houses: Bottengoms, Shadde-low's, Jocelyn's, Berewyk, Gobblecock Hall – this last prudishly excised, I notice, from the latest Ordnance Survey maps. And the place names: Assington Thicks and Tiger Hill, Workhouse Green and Honey Tye, Cripple Corner and Calais Street. You couldn't live here without sensing the half-heard murmurings of history, whispering out of the landscape itself.

Later on, I stumbled across other secrets in other corners of the county. At Easton, in the back country north of Wood-bridge, I watched the huntsman of the Easton Harriers cut up the bloated blue carcass of a flyblown, long-dead calf for his hounds. They encircled the grisly feast, tongues dripping. The stink almost made me vomit, but Steven Swan worked on regardless, talking of the hares he hunted with a deep under-standing that might have set any hunt saboteur back on his heels. It was a paradox familiar to those with their boots and hearts deep in the Suffolk clay.

At Tattingstone, down near the Essex border on the Shotley peninsula between Orwell and Stour, I found the Orange Box, the smallest and plainest pub imaginable, with the warmest atmosphere. This is a rare survival, a genuine old Suffolk labourers' alehouse where piped music is banned and talk encouraged. People come in for a bit of conversation, a drop of decent beer, and perhaps a singsong if the mood is right. On the hill opposite stood the Tattingstone Wonder, a fine flint-built church to all appearances – until I wandered round to the back and saw that the tower was a hollow sham, the nave a cleverly disguised row of brick cottages. Edward White of Tattingstone Place built the Wonder in 1790, partly to house three of his estate workers' families, partly to give himself and his guests something nice to look at out of his drawing-room windows. Back in the Orange Box, the company mused on what their forebears might have said or sung there, two centuries before, concerning the whims and fancies of their master.

A last snapshot of rural Suffolk, from South Elmham up near the Norfolk border: a landscape virtually unchanged for a thousand years, of big open fields, commons and ancient woodlands scattered with tiny hamlets whose names are those of their Norman or early medieval churches – St James South Elmham, St Margaret South Elmham, St Peter South Elmham, All Saints South Elmham. And sunk in a wood, the ruined flint walls of the Minster, a church so old that the experts disagree on its date. It has probably been standing for well over thirteen hundred years. Was it, as stories say, the Saxon cathedral of the South Folk of Suffolk, their one shining light through the Dark Ages? There's no telling. The Minster crumbles on under ivy and birds' nests, another of East Anglia's half guessed, half hidden secrets.

To catch the full flavour of the Suffolk coast, you have only to listen to Benjamin Britten's music. Put on *Peter Grimes* or *Curlew River*, and there are the pounding rhythms of the North Sea, the rush and drag of waves on shingle, the cry of an oystercatcher and the moan of sea wind. Britten lived at Snape and then at Aldeburgh, getting inspiration from the eternal sounds of this exposed, bleak shore. There are places of refuge along the Suffolk coast, winding estuaries where sailing boats scud: the Orwell and Deben in the south, the long salt corridor of the Alde behind its ten-mile shingle spit, the narrow Blyth that widens into a broad saucer of mud-flats below the 'Cathedral of the Marshes', the great church of the Holy Trinity at Blythburgh. But shingle and marsh are the keynotes, from the remote hamlet of Shingle Street up through Minsmere and Walberswick to Southwold and far beyond.

Settlements along this coast are few, for a number of good reasons. The grim Martello towers at Bawdsey and Shingle Street, built against Napoleon, and the numerous Second World War pillboxes stand witness to the centuries-old threat of invasion. The giant shingle spit at Orford Ness shows what the sea can do to block off ports such as Orford, given time. And as for the destructive power of the North Sea – Dunwich is the classic exemplar of that. Friaries, churches, houses, market-place: all the fine buildings of the Middle Ages are gone beneath the waves, leaving only a handful of houses behind the shore and on the cliff, and a legend of golden bells heard tolling under the sea on stormy nights.

Norfolk is a place you can easily fall in love with, and many do – a life-long love affair with the big skies, the teeming bird life of the coast, the fabulous treasure of great flint churches, the slow-burning humour, the sense of being a very long way from the worst of modern life. This is another great squashed circle of a county, bedded on chalk and clay and flints, not quite as flat as its reputation would have you believe; a gently undulating, agricultural county with an almost hemispherical coastline, threaded by narrow lanes that lead to hidden farms or to nowhere, to a dead end on a low cliff or on the brink of a reedy marsh.

Wool underpinned Norfolk's medieval prosperity, and wool wealth built those wonderful churches. The flint-knappers, stonemasons and wood-carvers poured out their skills between the eleventh and fifteenth centuries, for love of God or of the gold of woolmasters and abbots. They let the clear Norfolk light flood into the churches through high clerestory windows; they built towards heaven, soaring towers set with pinnacles. Many of the villages that once clustered round the churches have shrunk away or vanished completely; as is the case at Salle, a few miles north-west of Norwich, where the fifteenth-century church of St Peter and St Paul stands majestically over a couple of cottages and the old village school. Salle gets my vote as Norfolk's finest parish church, for the intimate scale of the detail in its carvings and decorations, inside and out, as much as for the magnificence of its proportions and its sheer size.

The church builders of the Middle Ages were following a tradition laid down by their monastic predecessors. At Castle Acre in the west, at Binham Priory in the north, and at nearby Little Walsingham – goal of barefoot pilgrims down the centuries – you can wander among the ruins and remnants of their godly ambitions. The more worldly enterprise of rich laymen took shape in great country houses: the vast brick halls at Blickling and Holkham, for example. And around these palaces of God and man run the flinty, heavy fields ploughed by generations of Norfolk farmers and farm labourers, the bent backbone of the county.

Between Norwich and the eastern coast lie the Broads: ancient flooded peat diggings, where the marshmen of other ages fished, trapped wildfowl and cut reeds for thatch. These shallow lakes, interconnected by water channels and set in flat farmland, make ideal sheltered inland waterways for sailing and powerboating. And they are in serious trouble as a consequence. Their banks, eroded by boat wash, are crumbling. Their water has been thoroughly polluted by diesel oil from outboard engines, by phosphates from sewage-treatment plants, and by sulphate run-off and nitrate enrichment from the intensive agriculture of the farmlands around them. Half the Broads that existed a hundred years ago have disappeared, filled up to the brim with mud and carr woodland; of the forty or so that are left, at least thirty have become thick soups of sterile algae-choked water. What the Broads could be, and perhaps will be under the management schemes currently in place, are havens for wildlife. Hickling Broad Nature Reserve, a shining example of conservation management, has a bird list as long as your arm, including bearded tits, four kinds of warbler, flycatcher and reed bunting, marsh harrier and the booming-voiced, very rare and shy bittern. Here, too, you can see the splendid yellow swallowtail butterflies in summer, flapping like tropical birds about the reed beds and orchid meadows.

> *Pakefield for Poverty,*
> *Lowestoft for Poor,*
> *Gorleston for Pretty Girls,*
> *Yarmouth for Whores.*
> *Caister for Water Dogs,*
> *California for Pluck –*
> *But Bugger old Winterton,*
> *How Black she do look!*

Yarmouth could show more than whores, even in the days when that salty local jingle was common currency. As a stepping-off point for exploring the great smooth arc of the Norfolk coastline, East Anglia's premier seaside resort can be rowdy enough. But back across the town's narrow spit of land, sea captains' fine old houses look out on South Quay where the whalers and herring boats once lay so thickly you could walk dryshod across the river Yare. Caister has few water-dogs these days: but the 132-foot tower of Holy Trinity church at Winterton, a few miles up the coast, still looks pretty black from out at sea on a rough day.

It's well north of here, however, that the best of the county's sea margin begins. I have enjoyed Cromer as a summer weekend destination, especially around harvest when the famous poppies are in bloom along the cliffs. But put me on the marshes further to the west in the depths of a hard winter for the real thing, the sharp authentic bite of the North Norfolk coast. From the big windmill at Cley-next-the-Sea, by Blakeney's double-towered church and the boat quay at Wells-next-the-Sea, on through Burnham Overy Staithe and Brancaster to Holme-next-the-Sea and Hunstanton, then round the corner to west-facing Snettisham – here is a truly bleak coast, a succession of villages looking north towards the sea over the ever-expanding marshes that have cut them off from their former lifeblood of coastal trade. To those marshes, hundreds of thousands of wildfowl and waders come each winter – pink-footed and white-fronted geese, knot and dunlin, eider and wigeon. Out on the hooked shingle spit of Blakeney Point, grey plover and curlew pipe and whistle. At dusk the winter sky flushes pink and green, its flat sheets of colours pricked by swirling clouds and straggling Vs of birds, impelled by a mass collective impulse to make their way inland to roost. You walk slowly inland yourself at such an hour, to a hot meal in the wood-panelled Hoste Arms at Burnham Market, perhaps, or for a drop of cockle-warming, secret-recipe 'Nelson's Blood' in the Lord Nelson at Burnham Thorpe, the village where the hero of Trafalgar was born.

Standing on the shore below Snettisham on a clear day, you can look through binoculars across five or six miles of the

Wash's huge estuary – miles of water, or miles of mud and sandbanks, depending on the state of the tide – to a far-off line of marsh and sea wall down in the south-west. This is Lincolnshire's nethermost corner, a great wedge of land reclaimed from the sea, sheltering behind its protective wall; one of the elusive borders of East Anglia, a lonely end-of-the-world region of isolated hamlets marooned among enormous fields of corn, potatoes and narcissi. And south from here into Cambridgeshire wheels the million-acre disc of Fenland, where the skies are huger than any in Suffolk or Norfolk, the horizons flatter, the corn and beet prairies more gargantuan.

Great churches ride domed islands there; Dutch villages have drifted in from across the North Sea. The people are Fen Tigers and web-footed Yellowbellies; their beer tastes different, their houses lean backwards, there are swans in their gardens, their rivers and roads run twenty feet above their fields. Outsiders are strangers in Fenland, neither welcome nor unwelcome. Many turn their backs on this landscape, repelled by the unending rimless fields and the plain brick villages. Others are drawn magnetically in, fascinated by Fenland's otherworldliness, to spend a lifetime sifting the mysteries of this most secretive of the East Anglian outposts.

The Land of Lost Content

Walt Unsworth

That is the land of lost content,
I see it shining plain,
The happy highways where I went
And cannot come again

A.E. HOUSMAN
'A Shropshire Lad'

I try not to make a habit of falling off, but sometimes you just can't help it. I couldn't help it at Pontesford.

Pontesford Rocks lie on the side of Earl's Hill, a short distance out of Shrewsbury on the Bishop's Castle road. They are scenically splendid, with tall slabs and buttresses rising out of

186

tree-fringed slopes and a view across the Shropshire hills to take your breath away. The rock is almost as old as time itself: igneous, with sharp-cut holds that allow a firm grip, and though there's little friction to speak of, there isn't much to test the modern-day hard man. E2 grade at most and precious little even of that. Pontesford is for the tyro, or the modest climber who is something of a romantic. After all, Mary Webb, that most romantic of novelists, used to sit atop these rocks dreaming up the plot of *Gone to Earth*.

They had been discovered and climbed upon by Birmingham University climbers back in the thirties, then more thoroughly investigated by those two ace cragsmen Peter Harding and Tony Moulam after the war, followed by various climbers from Wolverhampton including yours truly.

It was fun climbing, really, and since the rocks rose in tiers of 200 feet there was plenty of room to play about. In particular, we were fascinated by a bold overhanging thrust of rock known as the Nose, high up on the East Buttress. Here was the route of the crag, Varsity Buttress, then regarded as severe, but since upgraded. It had an outstanding finish up Taylor's Crack, which involved a step sideways to the edge of all things, 200 feet clear of the ground; the very tip of the Nose. On first acquaintance it required a bold move, but once you knew the secret there was really nothing to it. Curiously, for such a well-documented route, nobody seems to know who Taylor was.

A deep and slippery gully separates the East Buttress from the West Buttress and the Pontesbury Needle. The Needle is a genuine one, with a pointy top and a steep face towards the valley fissured by a strenuous undercut chimney, which everyone tried to do elegantly for the simple reason that if you didn't it twisted your guts out. To the right of the chimney is a nasty-looking smoothly blank rib which, in those days, was the 'last great problem'. Completely unprotected, it was too difficult, too committing for our modest ambitions, and it took an expert gritstoner, Malcolm Baxter, to make the first ascent some time later. The Superdirect, as it is now called, is still a very bold lead. This was where Ed Drummond took the serious fall that is the basis for his well-known performance poetry.

But serious stuff like this was not the essence of Pontesford for us. Long sunny days on the slabs of West Buttress were more the norm and I particularly liked the great slab of Wall End, either by Wall End Climb or the trickier Finale Groove, two climbs that interlaced one with another right up the rocks, so you could pick 'n' mix your way to the top.

At one time the second pitch of Wall End Climb had to be either the Notch – a corner slit above a little slab like Amen Corner on Gimmer – or the ferocious overhanging crack that rightly belonged to Finale Groove. Both were much harder than the rest of the climb, which was a modest V. Diff. Pondering this one afternoon and not fancying either of the strenuous alternatives above me, I spied a small finger-hold on the wall above the slab and an equally small matching foothold. But only one of each, which is 50 per cent less than required.

I pottered up to investigate. The wall ended in a sharp arête away to the left. If there was a hold round the edge, all might be well, but I couldn't see round it. Squeezing the fingers of both hands into the nick in the wall I stepped across to the foothold then, hanging on, did a quick change of feet with a movement that would have graced the Royal Ballet. My left foot was now hanging uselessly in mid-air. Tentatively I let go with my left hand and leaning left, all the weight on my right foot and right fingers, groped round the corner. They call them 'Thank God' holds and, in this case, there was never a better name. My desperate digits curled round a magnificent great lovable incut hold. One pull and I was round the corner and soon at the next belay.

In those days I was a teacher and I happened to be climbing with one of my pupils, a strapping fifteen-year-old called John, who took to climbing like a monkey takes to coconuts. He was puzzled at first by the wall but when he made the move round the arête, his amazement at finding the perfect hold made him exclaim, 'Bloody hell!' Then, seeing his teacher sitting at the belay just above, he added, 'Sir.' A few years later John went on to make an early British ascent of the North Face of Piz Badile.

The problem with the Nose in those days was to force a direct route up the middle by an obvious weakness. It wasn't that easy, and the curse of Pontesford has always been the uncertain nature of the rock. Pieces come away without warning, sometimes after years of use, and particular care is needed on new ground.

One afternoon a large group from Wolverhampton were spread around the rocks, when a couple decided to make an attempt on the Nose Direct. I thought they might succeed, for they were skilled climbers, so I scrambled to a ledge below the Nose ready to photograph the action. The leader was soon struggling, his movements becoming desperate. Suddenly he lunged for a hold above him, grabbed it and pulled. The hold came away and almost in slow motion, it seemed, the climber began to slither down the rock. I shouted a warning, too late, of course, and then felt a stunning blow to the head. By incredible chance the loose piece of rock had hit me on the temple. There were no protective helmets in those days. The blow knocked me unconscious and I rolled over the edge of the crag . . .

★

Although I had begun my hillwalking at an early age, on the fells of the Lake District and the moors of the Pennines, when I went to live in the Midlands I soon became acquainted with the rolling hills of Shropshire. It is strange frontier country, with villages half lost in the mists of time, connected one with another only by the narrowest of roads. There's a hint of mystery, even of witchcraft, about the place and the tales of Wild Edric seem somehow feasible.

Edric was a Saxon thane who held these lands and resisted the Norman invasion. He was obviously a first-rate guerrilla leader – the Che Guevara of his day – and audacious to an astonishing degree, even burning down the half-completed castle the Normans were building at Shrewsbury. He became known as Wild Edric but in the end, realizing that the Normans were invincible, he adopted the well-known principle that if you can't beat 'em, join 'em, and became a Norman supporter.

The ghost of Edric haunts the Stiperstones, perhaps the best known of all Shropshire's hills, unique among the high places of England in that it consists of a swelling moor with a series of rock pinnacles marching across its top like a set of gigantic decaying molars. In appearance they are like a scaled-down version of a scene from the Dolomites – the Tre Clima, perhaps – but appearances deceive; no Dolomites these, but pinnacles of black shiny quartzite, which rattles to the touch and offers little in the way of climbing. Nevertheless, they are impressive, especially when seen through an autumn mist as evening falls and the spirit of the place takes hold of the imagination.

It is not surprising that such a bewitching place abounds in legends and superstition, especially the largest of the pinnacles, which is known as the Devil's Chair: fifty feet of shattered rock like a broken-down Norman keep. According to legend, the Devil dropped these rocks while flying over the moor one night

– a fairly common explanation for unusual rocks in the British countryside – but on this occasion he must have been carrying quite a load. When mist shrouds the rocks the Devil is said to be in his chair. Mary Webb described it in *Golden Arrow*.

So the throne stood – black, massive, untenanted, yet with a well-worn air . . . It was understood that only when vacant could the throne be seen. Whenever rain or driving sleet or mist made a grey shechinah there people said, 'There's harm brewing. He is in his chair.' Not that they talked of it much; they simply felt it, as sheep feel the coming of snow.

Superstition has it that anyone with a problem to solve should come up on the moor at midnight and dance round the Chair three times. If music is heard, the answer to the problem is *yes!* Since the Chair is surrounded by a field of large boulders, the answer is more likely to be a broken leg.

Another legend says that Wild Edric, his golden-haired wife, Lady Godda, and his warriors live beneath the rocks and appear on the eve of war riding towards the fateful dawn to save England. There have been numerous reported sightings. A miner and his daughter saw them pass when British troops sailed for the Crimea in 1854 – she described Edric as a dark man with short curly hair wearing a green cloak and coat and carrying a sword. The most recent sighting was on the eve of the Falklands War. The Stiperstones is not alone in this phenomenon, of course, though usually it is Arthur and his knights who are on underground duty, rather than Edric.

There's a car park at the southern end of the Stiperstones, below Cranberry Rock, and it is very easy to stroll up and scramble over each of the pinnacles in turn. The highest is Manstone Rock, at 1,759 feet (536 m) the second highest summit in Shropshire, just 13 feet (4 m) less than Brown Clee. There's a good track along the moor, leading from rock to rock, but off the path the going can be rough, with lots of big blocks and on the western side tangled bilberries, worth collecting in the season.

The view from any of the pinnacles – or even the moor itself – is very fine. To the west is the large cone of Corndon Hill, curious in shape and name, while beyond it is Offa's Dyke country. The Welsh border is scarcely two miles away. Over to the east is the East Onny vale, with Bridges and its famous pub and beyond that the swelling breasts of the Long Mynd. Pontesford can be seen, too, by the discerning eye: the last knoll before Shrewsbury.

You can walk down off the northern end of the moor to the Stiperstones Inn, through the remains of the lead-mining industry which was once so important here. The Romans mined for lead hereabouts and by 1870 this little area between Stiperstones and Corndon was producing 10 per cent of the country's lead ore. Miners established freehold cottages on the edge of Stiperstones, on common land, creating the little communities of Pennerley and Perkins Beach. The last mine closed in 1911. When I first came here in the fifties these places were much run-down, semi-derelict, and yet they had a strange beauty. Cornish miners were brought up to work the mines in the middle of the last century and built their distinctive tall engine houses, now gaunt ghosts against a leaden sky, and the land itself, on this side of the Stiperstones, is deeply cut into attractive dells. In recent years the growing interest in our industrial heritage has seen a revival of such places as Perkins Beach and old cottages have become the latest desirable residences.

I used to stay at the Stiperstones Inn on the occasional winter weekend and climb Stiperstones in the snow. There are some steep slopes and I remember vigorous bouts of step-kicking when the temperature was sharp but the sky above pure azure. I learned a lot about snow on these little ridges: its structure and consistency, what would hold and what wouldn't, how to kick a step with the minimum of effort, how to climb up, down and across it. Later, in the Alps and on the steep face of the Ben, such knowledge proved invaluable because I didn't have to worry about the snow. I knew exactly what it would do.

Away to the south of Stiperstones there are smaller, more intimate hills, separated one from another by deep and secret valleys. Little Hopesay Hill, above the village of the same name, is one such. It has a stunning view towards the Kerry Ridgeway, and the ancient fort of Burrow. The district is littered with these ancient earthworks and a favourite of mine is the one known as Bury Ditches, on a hill above Clun. I walked up here one day from the farm at Guilden Down (where, incidentally, the strongest British earthquake was recorded in 1990 – 5.4 on the Richter scale), through the woods, gaining height steadily, until the astonishing ditches burst into view. Unlike many of its kind Bury Ditches does not disappoint. It is the site of an Iron Age township. Two thousand years ago a couple of hundred people lived here and it looks as though they only left last week. You can see quite plainly what they were about and how they defended the place.

There's lots of poking about to be done on these lesser hills. What was it Kipling said?

> *Something hidden. Go and find it. Go and look behind*
> *the Ranges –*
> *Something lost behind the ranges. Lost and waiting for you.*
> *Go!*

I've always believed that there is more to mountains than just rock and ice, important though those are. There's a deeper affinity – something to do with the soul, I suppose – that makes my heart lift just as much when I see the Shropshire hills from Church Stretton or Bishop's Castle as when I see the Alps from Chamonix or Zermatt.

One day I walked from Bishop's Castle to Clun, first along the Kerry Ridgeway, with views of the remote Clun Forest – all famous sheep country – until I came to a sign indicating a footpath along Offa's Dyke. I followed the great ditch south for a couple of miles, wondering at its usefulness in days gone by. It was never a defensive position like Hadrian's Wall, but simply a boundary beyond which the tribes of the west dare not venture. It says a lot for Offa's power that he could just draw a line in the sand, and say to the Welsh, 'OK, boyo. Step beyond that and you get clobbered.' It was an Offa they couldn't refuse. A few did and for a first offence had a hand cut off; for a second offence their head was cut off and there is no recorded instance of a third offence.

The Dyke hereabouts is in very good condition, the two ditches and central embankment plain to see. All the peasants from round about – on the English side, at least – must have been dragged from their farms to lend a hand in its construction and they did a good job. I'll bet the M6 motorway doesn't last as long. The walking is very up and down, following the Dyke, with a really steep drop at Churchtown, into a narrow defile of a valley. Though there is a church here, there's no town; the 'town' being Mainstone, a hamlet, really, nearly a mile down the road. And the stone that gives Mainstone its name is a huge boulder weighing over a hundred kilos – only it isn't in the town, it's in the church. Clear?

I left the Dyke at a hill called Hergan and strolled over the long whaleback ridge of Cefns, climbing stile after stile into tight little Clun, with its magnificent Norman keep in a bend of the river.

All these hills are in the west of the county, but there are attractive hills in the east too, if not quite so wild: Caer Caradoc and Wenlock Edge, the Wrekin and Brown Clee. All part of Housman's 'blue remembered hills'. Between west and east rises the vast bulk of the Long Mynd, ten miles in length and three or four wide. It rises to 1,693 feet (516 m) and though it is fairly level on top, with an ancient road called the Portway running along it, it is surprisingly steep at the sides. On the eastern edge it is dissected by deep valleys known as batches, or hollows, which make immensely satisfying short walks – up one hollow to the Portway and down another.

The best centre for exploring the Long Mynd – and the Shropshire hills as a whole, come to that – is Church Stretton. It is easy to see why they call Church Stretton 'Little Switzerland': the hills crowd round and houses peep from the wooded slopes like chalets in an Alpine valley. The buildings climb up the slopes of the Long Mynd along an incredibly steep road called the Burway until they give up with a last gasp and leave the road to struggle up by itself. It is a narrow, twisting road all the way to Ratlinghope (pronounced Ratchup) in the next valley with some steep drops by its side. Something of a local test-piece in the early days of motoring, it is still not a joyous experience for nervous drivers. I well remember one night some friends brought me over the Burway in a blizzard, when driving snow cut visibility almost to zero and we crawled forwards, straining to see the road, conscious of deeper darknesses in the murk where the land dropped away. We were glad to reach the welcoming fire in the pub at Bridges and steady our nerves with a double malt.

The most popular walk on the Long Mynd is undoubtedly a stroll up the Carding Mill valley from Church Stretton. The old mill was used for carding or combing wool to get it ready for spinning, but that finished late in the last century when it turned to making mineral water. A century and a few changes later, it is now the National Trust tea room and shop.

Even as far as the mill, the valley is attractive, steep-sided and with a lively stream, but beyond the mill it becomes wilder and narrower, like a clough in the high Pennines. It steepens too, and if you think the going is rough, which it is, then consider what it must have been like before the 1850s when Dr Charles Mott raised a public subscription to have it improved. It is known as Mott's Road in his honour. No doubt the doctor used it on his rounds to the isolated farms round Ratlinghope.

In winter, in the old days, crossing Long Mynd was always fraught with danger. The snow could lie deep, and the fair held in Church Stretton just before Christmas was known as Dead Man's Fair because several farmers and drovers had perished returning from it across the moor. One man's adventure is well recorded: that of the Rev. Donald Carr whose crossing of the Long Mynd during the great storm of January 1865 became legendary. Carr was the rector of Woolstaston on the north-eastern edge of the Long Mynd and he also looked after the little church at Ratlinghope, on the other side of the moor, about four miles away. Sunday, 29 January 1865 was a day on which deep snow was lying on the Long Mynd but Carr had crossed the moor in all weathers and this perhaps made him a little over-confident. He struggled through knee-deep snow and head-high drifts, until he reached Ratlinghope, performed a short service for the few parishioners who had braved the weather and set off back for his six o'clock service at Woolstaston.

The wind rose and with it came stinging sleet. Before long the parson was lost, floundering through deep snow, falling into ravines, hands and feet frozen. Darkness fell and he staggered through the night, convinced that if he went to sleep he would die in the snow. He hoped that dawn would bring relief but the moor was draped in mist and, to add to his difficulties, he rapidly became snow-blind. His boots came off and he struggled on in stockinged feet. By sheer chance he found himself in the Carding Mill valley where he was discovered, barely alive, by some children, his hair and clothes matted in ice. He had been walking over the moor for twenty-two hours.

Donald Carr gave a lecture on his adventure, which was later published as a booklet called *A Night in the Snow*. Surprisingly, it is still in print and readily available in Church Stretton. The detailed description that Carr gives of his remarkable experience makes it well worth reading, even today, and especially by mountaineers and hill-walkers. Quite a few of us might put hands on heart and mutter, 'There but for the grace of God . . .'

I found myself plummeting down Pontesford's East Buttress in jolting bounds as I bounced off the rock. A friend said later that he thought I'd thrown my red sweater down the crag, not realizing that I was still inside it. I must have regained consciousness quickly because I was able to watch myself falling. It was a strange experience: I was completely outside my body watching it fall. There was no fear, just a feeling of 'Poor devil, he's had it,' as though it was some stranger I was watching. It was 150 feet to the ground, which I knew was approaching rapidly.

Like King Charles, I was saved by an oak tree: I crashed through the thick foliage, which broke what would otherwise have been a fatal fall. I came round in Shrewsbury Infirmary,

with a broken ankle and several cracked vertebrae, which im-
mobilized me for the next six weeks.

As luck would have it I was due to leave the Midlands for a
new job up north, so I saw less of the Shropshire hills after
that. But I have been back from time to time. I even went
back to Pontesford – to climb the Nose Direct and write the
guidebook. I felt it owed me that, at least.

AVON CALLING
Stephen Venables

Mountaineers are supposed to love the wild places and of course I do. The silent crags of Torridon, the empty vastness of Tibet, the pristine clarity of Snow Lake, the Gothic spires of Patagonia . . . all these have moved me intensely and yet one of my favourite climbing haunts is a squalid little quarry above a main road on the edge of one of Britain's major cities.

I went there recently to celebrate my fortieth birthday. It was a Sunday in May and we had three hours to spare before a lunch party at home in Bath – just time to drive into Bristol for a quick climb. The A4 was jam-packed and it took ages to fight our way through Brislington's shapeless suburbs, into the urban heart of Temple Meads and on through the post-industrial turmoil of Fishponds to a concrete maze of badly signposted flyovers, designed specifically to harass tense drivers. But by now we had almost arrived, and as we came round a corner, there was the sight which always gives a thrill of expectancy: Brunel's famous bridge, flanked by towering cliffs of Regency architecture – an absurd, bombastic, theatrical foil to the real focus of the picture, which is the natural cliff of pale limestone supporting the right-hand tower of the bridge. And as you drive closer into the gorge, the vista opens to reveal further cliffs rising 200 feet and more from the oily brown sluice of the Avon. They are shaped unmistakably by the quarryman's dynamite and chisel and yet, after decades of weathering, these cliffs have a grandeur that defies the polluted water and traffic below.

We chose a comparatively easy climb that birthday morning – a Hard Very Severe route called Giant's Cave Buttress. I had not done the route for nearly twenty years and as we romped up it, finding the moves easier than they had ever seemed in youth, I banished worries about mid-life crisis. The rock was warm, rough and friendly and, despite the roar of traffic below and the gawpers staring sullenly from the man-made cave, there was an incongruous feeling of wilderness – an urban wilderness where wallflowers migrate from their bourgeois gardens to jostle with craggy valerian, and semi-naturalized fennel and parsley colonize crevices among the wild thyme, all flourishing in a hot-scented botanical paradise. In the gully beside us, the whitebeam shone silver amid black yew and the first translucent unfurlings of beech. Everything sang the joy of spring, celebrating my first rock climb of the season, and reaffirming my affection for a crag that, over the years, has become a familiar friend.

★

It was not always like that. My first visit to 'The Gorge' was on a dank November day in 1973. I had only been climbing a year or so and in that grey light the urban crag was oppressive and frightening. The serried overhangs of Main Wall seemed impossibly steep. In any case, this was a university meet and I had been asked to take care of a novice Frenchman called Pierre, so I chose the comparatively gentle line of the classic Piton Route. Movement warmed numb fingers and success calmed my fear, so afterwards I asked Pierre if he would like to try something a little harder. He agreed and we scrambled up through a bramble thicket to the foot of Suspension Bridge Arête.

The Suspension Bridge cliff, unlike most of the Gorge, is natural unquarried limestone – steep, fingery and unforgiving of shoddy technique. The Arête was my first ever HVS climb and perhaps it was rash to attempt it on a cold November afternoon with a novice, but climbing, in my book, was always supposed to involve a bit of a struggle. It was only as I grappled with the crux chimney that I began to regret the struggle, to hate the awful dry-throated fear, the trembling legs, the sooty smell of cold, unyielding stone bruising my numb hands. I shook and wobbled, fumbling unsuccessfully with nuts, tangling slings around my neck, blowing in a gasping frenzy to bring the aching heat of life back to clawed fingers. They managed finally to thread a sling though an old rusty peg and clip in the rope, which gave me the courage to make one final terrified lunge to the top of the climb.

In those days there was no giant bolt at the top of the Arête. There were trees round the corner but I wanted to belay at the edge, in contact with my novice second. So I hammered a peg into a hairline crack. In my ignorance, this single, knife-blade peg seemed sufficient, certainly adequate to bring up a second.

Standing at the top, I was euphoric, savouring the sweet after-taste of victory, thrilled with the success of my first HVS climb and wondering idly which of three different parties I might go to that night, back in Oxford. I was also paying close attention to the rope, bracing myself to help Pierre, who was obviously struggling, out of sight on the wall below. For some reason I did not have my belay gloves, so I was particularly careful to keep the rope taut in my bare hands. Pierre was shouting, but I couldn't hear his words above the traffic. He seemed to be reversing a section, so I paid out the rope carefully, unaware that he was still climbing, having failed to unclip the rope from the peg in the chimney. The spectator-ghouls on the bridge had gathered to watch every move, but from my perch I could not see Pierre teetering out on to the right-hand wall, dragging more and more slack rope. When eventually his fingers uncurled and he fell from the rock, there were twenty feet of slack rope between him and the peg.

It was like a cruel joke. The rope suddenly whipped me forward, feet skidding on gravel, hands trying to clench the searing nylon. I can still remember the metallic 'ping!' as the peg was plucked from its crack. I can recall precisely the terrible, shocked disbelief as I felt myself lurching forward, out into the void, unaware that the rope was still clipped into the peg in the chimney. In classic slow motion I floated in space, staring down at a green blur of grass and brambles – my death, waiting for me, just over a hundred feet below. This was it – this absurd, ridiculous moment of suspended time, taking me, unprepared, after only nineteen years.

I never hit the ground. I just became aware of bouncing and sliding and opening my eyes to realize, with intense, delighted surprise, that I was alive, hanging about thirty feet above the ground. The rope stretched up taut to the old rusty peg in the chimney, about sixty feet above me, then back down to Pierre, who had stopped about three feet off the ground. The man I had nearly killed was, thank God, completely unhurt, saved by three inches of rusty steel. I had a dislocated shoulder and a bloody broken knee, which must have taken a glancing blow in mid-flight. There was also a powerful smell of burnt flesh and nylon and as I held up my left hand I found deep grooves etched into the shiny pink skin of my fingers. Luckily they quickly turned numb in the cold, but the knee and shoulder remained obstinately painful.

The rescue was hilarious but humiliating. I half sat, half lay on a narrow ledge, moaning with pain and cold, while the police insisted on trying to lower a stretcher on steel hawsers from the top of the cliff. Only after two hours, when they had finally admitted defeat, were two highly competent climbers who had come over from an adjoining route allowed to get me down to a more realistic, land-based stretcher at the bottom of the cliff. By now the press had arrived in force. It was Sunday night and there was nothing much else on offer for the evening news, so I was carried down into a blazing circus of television lights and thrusting microphones. Shivering with cold and pain, angry, embarrassed and humiliated, I reacted with adolescent hostility. My curses were eliminated from the soundtrack, but everyone who watched the news that night recognized my old black and white Norwegian jersey, with the leather elbow patches, gesticulating angrily as I thrust V signs at the television cameras.

I don't think Pierre ever climbed again. I did, but over a year passed before I returned to the Gorge. On that test visit I was understandably nervous and it was ironic that my companion, Geoffrey Grimmett, chose Hell Gates, another route on the Suspension Bridge Buttress. Geoffrey climbed well; I dithered.

Self-esteem sank to its lowest ebb on the traverse into the famous Hell Gates Cave, where there was then a book recording every ascensionist's name. As I fumbled my way through a sequence of wrong moves, Geoffrey shouted delightedly, 'Listen to this: "November 3rd, 1973. I was sitting here when suddenly some loony lobbed off the top of Suspension Bridge Arête. If you are the loony and you have got this far, be more careful this time. Dave Hermelin."'

I *was* more careful and, after that initial rebuff, the Gorge began to seem a friendlier place. Later that term I led Central Buttress, spurred on by shouts of encouragement from local boy Andy Brazier. This was more typical Avon quarried rock – strange blocky stuff, with few obvious cracks and holds. You could have the strongest arms in the world and fail here. But, if you trusted rubber friction on slopy holds and used your hands to pinch and push and lean on sideways edges, you could discover a whole new world of deliciously precarious balance.

That summer, 1975, was my last term at Oxford, and I escaped several times from the tedium of revision to visit our local crag in Bristol. The council had closed the A4 Portway for one of its periodic spells of loose-rock removal and, without traffic, the Gorge was transformed into a peaceful haven where I began to appreciate the myriad trees, shrubs and flowers flourishing in the limestone. At last I ventured on to Main Wall, to do Mercavity, marvelling at the bold vision of Bonington, who had pioneered this first breach of Main Wall's defences in the sixties. And then, of course, we had to climb Bonington's later, more famous route, Malbogies, right up the centre of the wall.

I was going well, and one Saturday morning I arrived in the Gorge knowing that it was going to be a special day. Brimming with the confidence of youth, focused, determined, ambitious, I had decided to stick my neck out and do my first 'Extreme'. Lich Gates was the route, and as I began to grapple with the subtle meanderings of its first pitch, seeking out the rock's improbable weaknesses, clipping protection slings to pitons and old quarrymen's stakes, I thrilled to that rare sensation of everything flowing and fitting easily into place. The second pitch was harder, but it wasn't going to stop me – not even the final traverse, where I had to tiptoe so carefully, teetering sideways, fingering the wall above for tiny edges to hold my body in balance, until I could reach into the final shallow groove and bridge up to the top, to belay triumphantly on the park railings, casting disdainful looks at the promenaders who dared to stare at my incongruous helmet and karabiners.

My partner on Lich Gates was Bill Stevenson, with whom I later did my first alpine winter climbing. He was ascetic to a fault, with a manic gleam in the eye. Even more manic, but in a different league, far out of my reach, was Dave Ivory, whose new route Captain Swing was then reputed to be one of the hardest in the Gorge. Other Oxford companions of that era included Steve Parr, who took me up Pink Wall Direct and who later disappeared in the Himalaya. Roger Everett, the most consistently talented, was patient enough to hold my rope while I dithered for over an hour on the dubiously protected crux of Krapp's Last Tape, exhibiting all the negativity of Beckett's turgid anti-hero, before finally committing myself to an improbable shuffle on sloping nothingness, salvaging a crumb of respect from the man who had agreed to accompany me on my first Himalayan expedition later that year.

Krapp's Last Tape was in 1977 – the same year that I first ventured into the Gorge's most exclusive corner, the giant, carbuncular yellow walls behind Unknown Buttress. Steve Parr led the first pitch of The Blik, weaving balancy moves between overhanging walls; then I led the soaring top pitch, stopping to rip out the rotting remains of an old wooden wedge and slot in its place a large alloy hexentric – one of a hundred little visual details that stick in the memory. Many years later I returned to climb The Blik with its original author, Ed Drummond. Perhaps it was the effect of being with one of the great Avon pioneers, or perhaps I had just improved; whatever the reason, I seemed to flow up the route with infinitely greater ease. It was the same, one November morning, nipping into the Gorge for a quick session on the Suspension Bridge Buttress with two other Avon pioneers, Chris Bonington and Derek Walker: when you are with the old masters you daren't dither, for fear of losing face.

In recent years, living in Bath, the Gorge had been even closer to home – a place to escape to for a moment's heightened intensity, like the morning when I drove in to take some photos and ended up soloing Malbogies, knowing, as I reached over the key overhang, that if I messed this up I would fall to my death. On another occasion, soloing Great Central, I nearly panicked on the crux nose, eighty feet above the ground, cursing the polished sheen on the crucial holds, forcing myself to breathe deep and concentrate, extracting every available ounce of limited friction. It was frightening, but the reward was glorious, as I completed the moves in a cathartic life-affirming surge of triumph and continued to the pure, fearless enjoyment of the top pitch, before racing round for a final romp up Suspension Bridge Arête, the route that had given so much grief back in 1973.

Solo climbing has a unique intensity, but the best climbs in the Gorge have been gentler affairs, shared with friends. Most enjoyable were summer evenings with Keith Cartwright and others, racing to see how much mileage we could fit in, often finishing in the dark, rushing back down through black face-whipping undergrowth to the car park, then speeding over to Hotwells for the obligatory ritual pint or three at the Plume of Feathers, revelling in the pub's unashamed seediness. There have been so many other memorable days and evenings: triumphing on the edgy crux of Drang, one spring day on the way back from Wales; meeting Victor Saunders for the first time on the same route, little realizing that many years later he would save my life in the Himalaya; dithering for two long, long summer evenings on the crux of Peryl, dreaming of returning one day, with more courage, to complete the magnificent first pitch; climbing the soaring line of Unknown Buttress, back in 1975, knowing that soon it would be pulled down and consigned to oblivion by the ever-zealous council; following a bumptious Brummy called Rod one cold Sunday morning up the improbable weavings of Pink Wall Direct, giving myself the fright of my life – and him the laugh of his life – when a jackdaw popped squawkily out of a crucial deep hold, nearly taking me with it.

The jackdaw incident was one of the few occasions where I have felt out of control. In the Gorge, generally, the great joy is that you are *in* control. Because the protection is sparse you cannot afford to fall off leading. You make a point of being in control, pondering carefully each delicate move, savouring the uniquely subtle nature of Gorge climbing, where the old cliché about 'defying gravity' has a particular aptness. The one occasion I felt completely out of my depth, I made sure that I was seconding. My partner, Brian Davison, led what we thought was the easiest line up the huge Unknown Wall. The second pitch involved the most precarious long reach, poised immediately above a vicious old quarryman's iron stake. The penalty for failure seemed to be a re-enactment of the death of Edward II. As for the brutal overhanging top pitch, it felt like dusty, flaky old corrugated cardboard and Brian had to haul me every inch of the way. Only afterwards did I discover that we had actually climbed a mixture of Captain Swing and Amanita Muscarina, routes which had both had a ferocious reputation when they were first climbed, back in the early seventies.

The following summer (1991), armed with a guidebook, I returned to lead the correct easier line up the Unknown Wall – Yellow Edge. It was a Sunday in June. My first son had been born three days earlier and I had the morning free to celebrate. Geoffrey Grimmett, the man who had given me such grief on Hell Gates back in 1975, agreed to come and hold my rope. He had hardly climbed for years, but he seemed agreeable to following me up quite a serious E3 route. Perhaps he thought that a new father should be indulged. Perhaps my new status gave me extra confidence. I don't know, but it seemed to be one of those days where everything flows. Even a short fall on the first pitch, when a flake broke loose, didn't seem to shake my confidence and on the second pitch I delighted in the delicate moves over the bulge, knowing that I was going to succeed. Geoffrey joined me for the most awkward changeover at a wild and improbable hanging belay, then watched intently as I started up the final pitch. Straight up left were the over-hanging corrugations where I had struggled after Brian the previous summer; out to the right was the easy ramp of Yellow Edge, which we had completely missed. Way, way out right it went, temptingly easy, but suspended above an immense drop, until it ended in space, at which point another ramp led back left all the way to the top of the cliff. Just like the classic 1938 route up the Eigerwand, this route up Avon's biggest wall followed the line of least resistance, zigzagging at a reasonable angle between 'impossible' overhangs. As with so many memorable classic routes, the individual moves were actually quite easy, but the overall situation was stupendous. For me, it was one to savour; for Geoffrey, following five minutes later as a summer thunderstorm burst over Bristol, it was more a matter of survival. By the time he reached the final moves, liquid red mud was splashing from the holds. Numb, shivering and bedraggled, he clawed desperately at the glistening rock, while I hauled on the rope, and together we dragged him out from the void, thrilled to have escaped in the nick of time.

Like so many of the best climbs Yellow Edge was a snatched opportunity – a glorious gift, enjoyed suddenly and spontaneously. The Avon Gorge, more than any other crag or mountain I know, seems to encapsulate that quality. By its very nature, at the heart of a city, close to working life, ambivalent, incongruous, half tame, half wild, it reflects all the joyful, intense, escapist rewards of rock climbing. For me it will always be a special place. Just like the first view of Tryfan from the A5, or the Buchaille appearing over the top of Rannoch Moor, or the first glimpse of the Jungfrau from the Lauterbrunnen road, the sight of Bristol's dear old eccentric Avon Gorge will always give me the same familiar thrill of recognition and expectancy.

A DREAM COME TRUE

John Wyatt

All of us who have a taste for adventure feel that somewhere out there beyond the haze of the horizon is the place where we should be. In our wildest imaginings it could be among the Isles of the Blest, or the Plains of Happiness; the rustic bliss of some unspoilt Arcady, or some hidden Shangri-la in the hollow of the everlasting hills. It is as if before we were born we came from some glorious place, and yearn for it. It is a sort of dream-nostalgia; a puzzling quest. It drives some of us to the outermost corners of the world; to its highest peaks, and to the most inhospitable places. Most of us accept that we can never quite reach our ideal because we know that it exists only in our dreams.

But dreams can become hope, hope can be a driving force, and hope sometimes can become reality. I never knew what to expect when I first came to the Lake District. I had camped and back-packed as a young member of the church's scout troop and I revelled in it. The hills within reach of the Lancashire cotton town where I was raised were great, but did not quite match the ideal that I was reading about in the adventure books borrowed from our local library. I hoped that one day, just over the next summit, it could be there. But it was that very special year when we worked hard to raise the cash to get to the camp near Windermere. Windermere? It was the other side of the world! The Lake District? Something seen on railway posters. It was, of course, raining when we arrived.

But it was on the days following that I felt the impact. I was stunned. Here, at last, it seemed I was near to what I had read and dreamed about. Where we camped I saw magnificent trees, taller than imagination. And then the shock of the view from an airy vantage point, lit by the muted light of evening: mountains shoulder to shoulder, crowding the horizon as far as my eyes could see. Below my feet the levels of the lake shining like burnished metal. And everything so clean and clear. Magic! It was as if even the air was aglow with light. This could not be real. I was dreaming! To recapture that memory I have returned happily to that place time and time again.

Helvellyn – there is a name to fire enthusiasm for the adven-turer. That, of course, had to be my first mountain. The ascent was made in fog, but no matter: it emphasized the height – I was up among the clouds! There, on the memorial to the dog that stayed faithfully by his dead master's side for three months, I read the words of Scott, which I could immediately remember and which have rolled off my tongue ever since:

> *I climbed the dark brow of the mighty Helvellyn*
> *Lakes and mountains beneath me gleamed misty and wide*
> *All was still save by fits when the eagle was yelling*
> *And starting around me the echoes replied.*

The mist made Striding Edge all the more exciting. I was walking in the clouds. I could not see what was below. To a young lad's imagination it was a thousand feet of cliff on either side. Then suddenly the memorial to Dixon, who met his end nearby. Then down below the clouds an incredible view of Ullswater. Since that day I have climbed the fell more times than I can count, in all weathers, fine and extreme, and day and night, because I have wanted to, sometimes because I had to. But it remains for me, in spite of being scorned by so many for its over-popularity, a very great friend. The crags of Helvellyn introduced me to so many adventures in the hills and forests and mountains at home and abroad.

Then it happened. Incredibly, at sixteen, what I keenly hoped for and sought became reality – a job and a home in the Lake District. It was a hands-on job, learning and working in woodland; axe, pick, shovel and saw. I could hardly believe my luck. I loved every moment – even back-breaking, soaking-wet moments. And on the free days I was out on my bike among the awesome hills and crags. Wordsworth regretted that the grown man loses the vision and excitement of youth. Perhaps I have yet to grow up because it has hardly happened to me. Trips to other outstanding natural areas of the world may have thrilled me, but have not made me less excited about what is here on my doorstep.

Later I had even greater, unbelievable luck. A career that gave me opportunity to help in the urgent and necessary task of conserving what I had grown to respect even more: the 880 square miles of the Lake District National Park.

I am often asked to name my favourite part of the Lake District, and have always wondered how to answer. Why so? I can say 'wherever I am at the time', but that is an easy let-out, if not really dishonest.

To me the Lake District is a magnificent collection of favourite places, each precisely where each belongs. The volcanic crags of the central fells can only be where they are within the ring of the waves of the sedimentaries. The sixteen lakes can only be where they are, close within the arms of the fells. The old hill farms, the human adaptation to the unpromising environment, are where they really belong and look as if they have grown out of the landscape. How can I choose any particular place?

A short walk from where I live brings me to a lake shore and a classic view across the sheet of tree-fringed water to the brows and crests and domes of the fells and the two pillars of the Pikes of Langdale. Such stunning views are repeated throughout Lakeland. They have a special quality. And their secret is that so much is packed into so little. Crammed into each scene is everything to capture the eye and tempt the explorer. The base of the fells stands near sea level, and their shapes and their crowding suggest fierce heights when only four summits are a little above 3,000 feet. Norman Nicholson, the Lakes poet, said that the Lake District is a confidence trick. So it is. The Pikes that I see could be twice as high. Distance is deceptive, perspective distorted. A trick – but a magnificent one!

The climbs are surprisingly accessible. Unlike other hill areas there are no weary miles of rough approach. A fit competent map-reading walker can accomplish any ascent to the highest peaks, or reach his climbing crag, and return to his starting point comfortably in a day, with a pleasing sense of achievement.

I have always felt, as others have, that on reaching a height my eye is captivated by the views of the other challenges around. I must one day climb this one, and that one. It is as if the more you climb, the more you crave. You develop an appetite for mountains. It requires satisfaction. It is as well, though, not to be greedy. I have nothing in common with those who would treat the fells and crags as a sort of outdoor gymnasium. I am seldom in a hurry. I have always felt that wild places need to be savoured.

What is a source of constant delight to me has attracted legions of artists for two centuries and, in latter years, photographers. It is the way the Lakeland scenes change with the moving light of day, with drifting cloud shadows hour by hour, and with the round of seasons. When the tops are touched with snow, as they can be through May, the scene is alpine and can match any such views anywhere. And on the tops then, with a cold east wind, the clarity of the panoramas is tremendous – north into Scotland, west to Man, south to Wales, east to the Pennines. And the air keen, invigorating, like good wine. In the fierce winter of 1962, when Windermere froze so hard that motorists drove on to the ice, one could have been in the Arctic Circle. And what about autumn? The warm reds and browns and yellows of broadleaved woods.

Well, of course, it rains. There are heavier falls in the central fells than in any other place in England, but thinning out the further one goes east and south. There are no more rainy days here than in most other parts of Britain; there is just more of it when it comes. I have seen it in flood when the deluge bounces huge boulders down the rivers with a noise like an artillery barrage. I have seen becks, pouring down the fell side, explode when dams of flood debris finally burst. And I have had to work in the rain, and even venture into it in darkness in the search for some wayward fell walker. And I have cursed rain like anyone else when it persists longer than it should, or has come at some inconvenient time. But I have had to remind myself – with tiresome regularity – that it is water that has made, and maintains, the Lake District's beauty. Like any Cumbrian outdoor worker I have had to shrug it off. 'Nay! Give o'er! It's nowt but a bit o' watter.'

Which is my favourite fell? If one loves best that which he has experienced with the sweat of his brow then I must again admit to Helvellyn. The biggest task there was to repair the dry-stone wind shelter near the summit. Not only was it suffering from the weather, walkers were removing stone to sit on, or sometimes even pathetically making a cairn to hide their litter. It was a mess. We had to rebuild – using hidden cement to keep it tight. No funds. No helicopters. Tons of sand and cement had to be humped to the summit from the Glenridding mine area, and water carried from the spring on the western slope. Scores of volunteers – the park's voluntary wardens, climbing and walking clubs, students, the Army, pony trekkers, any passing fell walker who could be persuaded – had to carry the bags weighing thirty pounds upwards, up the fell, weekend after weekend, and sometimes two trips in the day. I thought the job had finally done for me on the last day when I found myself really struggling to the summit – until I found that a joker had put an extra bag into my rucksack. Meanwhile, other volunteers, with skilled supervision, were building the shelter. The weather was patchy, sometimes high wind and rain, but when it was fine we could occasionally relax and enjoy clear views over most of the hills and mountains 'misty and wide': the mass of the Coniston Old Man range, the instinctive Pikes of Langdale, the jagged ridge of Crinkle Crags, tent-like Bow-fell, the Scafells – the highest land in England – the massive dome of Great Gable, Pillar, the Buttermere and Crummock fells, then Bassenthwaite Lake before the hump of Skiddaw and its neighbour Blencathra, the High Street Range, and Fairfield. And the seas: Solway Firth before the Scottish Gallo-way fells to the north, Morecambe Bay to the south.

There was a similar task at Stickle Tarn in the Langdales. The park owned the tarn and it was necessary to repair and improve the dam with more sand and cement. I have trudged up that lovely old zigzag to the tarn more times than I can tell. Carrying up, once leading pack-ponies, and sometimes helping carry stretchers down with the Langdale Mountain Rescue Team. One of my most enjoyable walks is up to the tarn, then beyond up on to the strangely named Sergeant Man, 2,414 feet (736 m) and as near to dead centre of the fells as one can get. A nice airy place in summer, and great in the winter with snow crunching under boots. Then off by High Raise and across the wide open moor – skylarks here in summer! To the Pikes themselves, the strange thumb of Pike o' Stickle, and the tooth of Harrison Stickle, and down the path by the side of the deep hollow gash of Dungeon Ghyll; a path on which Captain Budworth, the eighteenth-century fell walker, had to have a scarf tied over his right eye to avoid being overcome by the horror of seeing the drop into the chasm on that side. I remem-ber an apprehensive step by step down the path once when it was unexpectedly covered in smooth sheet ice.

Is my favourite fell the highest? Scafell Pike has many mem-ories and continues to attract me. It is the most popular fell summit after Helvellyn because it happens to be the highest place in England (3,210 feet/977 m). I have never been alone on the summit but have found myself in conversation with folk from all over the world. But most miss the exploration of the rest of the massif. There is Scafell itself, separated from its higher brother by the gap of Broad Stand, a minor rock climb, and in spite of warnings in guidebooks and hostel posters, over the years the cause of many accidents to the uninitiated walker. But then on the Pike's massif there is Broad Crag, Lingmell and Ill Crag, all worthy summits; and there are hollows and gullies and ravines where I have enjoyed searching for alpines, or just sitting eating my butties away from the crowds.

Across to the north from the Pike is the awesome enormity of Great Gable. Well named it is, but with a gable end that nothing man-made could match. I can recall with gratitude some great climbing days on the crags of its eastern flank. Here again the fell is so popular that the footpaths, crumbling under the weight of numbers, have been restored. On a recent visit the summit was occupied by an organized party of Americans, who seemed to be looking forward to a sumptuous picnic at Styhead Tarn. A good place for it. It used to be said that there, at the cross-roads of the fells, if one stayed long enough (eating?) every mountaineer in the world would walk by. But that was in the days when mountaineering was in its infancy and most of its enthusiasts were British. It is now entertaining to me to watch all the cosmopolitan world and his wife and children walk by. Many, having struggled in an effort to get there, modify their intentions and decide that the Pikes, or Gable, might be climbed another day.

A favourite valley? When the roads are swarming with a serious infestation of cars in high season the valley of the Duddon would be my choice to get away from most of it. When I was asked to help make a radio programme that featured all the sounds of Lakeland, from the sea on the shore, to running water, farmland, quarry, and fell, where else could I choose? Dunnerdale has everything except a natural lake. At its foot the sea at Duddon Sands, which are criss-crossed by ancient roads only passable at low tide. Following the river upwards there are waterfalls and pools, and farmsteads and old quarries, the wildlife abundant, and quiet, remote heights around.

On a countryside expedition I am loath to see too many signs of human activity. I remember being angry at finding a wooden stile on a fell-top wall – wooden when there was so much loose rock around! And a National Trust by-law sign on another. (No longer there!) And a profusion of misleading cairns built by – who? They grow like mushrooms! But in the valleys, particularly here in the Duddon, there are signs of human enterprise I admire. Near Duddon Bridge, where the modern road crosses the river, a piece of hauntingly interesting industrial archaeology: the beautifully preserved stone-built water-powered blast furnace, abandoned in the eighteenth century when fuel ran out. Prime iron ore from the Furness mines was brought up the Duddon on the tide by barge. Charcoal came from the woods for miles around until hardly a tree remained. You can imagine the vast quantities of charcoal needed by observing the height of the charcoal store. There, a stone wall has been turned to glass from a time when the fuel accidentally caught fire. To produce such an amount of charcoal would have meant unbelievable quantities of coppice wood, cut and collected, and carefully baked day and night by men who worked hard and long, and lived hard by their fires.

Then up the wooded banks to Ulpha, with its ancient Angle name (meaning Wolf hill), past the Penn, a hill that retains its Celtic name; and past Ulpha a minor road comes down into the valley from Broughton Mills. Just up that road is a dry-stone wall, which is incredible! Bear in mind that every stone had not only to be lifted and carried, but shifted around and manoeuvred precisely into position. The enormous size of the stones here must mean that it was built by a waller of tremendous strength. Who was this super-human giant? I once took a skilled waller to the spot and he was speechless. Further up the delectable valley is another high path-side dry-stone wall under Harter Fell. This, too, is astonishing to me: it is so well made that you can hardly get a blade of a knife through any joint. It not only makes me ashamed of my efforts at building but amazed at the craftsmanship. Its creator was the Michelangelo of walling!

One can hardly think of Dunnerdale without being reminded of Wonderful Walker, mentioned by Wordsworth and others. For sixty-six years he was curate-in-charge at the little church at Seathwaite in the eighteenth century with a stipend of five pounds per annum, and made ends meet with farm work. He also ministered to and counselled his flock, and taught the local children. He and his wife raised a family and at his death he left two thousand pounds in his will. A good example to all hard-working Victorians? A saint? He must have had some faults.

The river cuts under the climbing crag of Wallowbarrow. Then at the valley head there is Grey Friar fell of the Coniston Old Man range on the east, and the gem of Harter Fell on the west. Harter is, indeed, only a little above two thousand feet but it repays a flog up through the conifer forest (created against opposition from conservationists in the 1930s). The highest point is on one of several outcrops and the view is extensive from the Scafells to the north and Langdales in the south. But a walk and a scramble around to the north brings another view of astonishing human achievement. The Roman fort of Mediobogdum was built during the reign of the Emperor Hadrian. The remains of its walls and exercise ground are clearly seen on its fell-side ledge high in Eskdale. I find it amusing, having suffered under meaningless regulations in the services, that this was built to the rule-book plan – even though its north-west gate opens on to a cliff face! Here in this exposed place, with wonderful views of the highest land in England, infantry and cavalry from a cohort originating in Dalmatia, in former Yugoslavia, patrolled the zigzag road from the fort at Ambleside, through the fells over Wrynose and Hardknott Passes, then down Eskdale to the fort and port at Ravenglass. How did the men live here? They even had their bathhouse. Where did they enjoy recreation? I return to this place time and time again, and Kodak have done quite well from my photographic attempts to capture its magic.

From Harter I must descend into Eskdale. Up the valley from Harter, upper Eskdale is one of the remotest areas among the central fells. Once a deer forest, Great Moss belonged to the monks of Furness Abbey. From here is the most dramatic but the trickiest of the ascents up Scafell or the Pike by the side of the ravine of Cam Spout. Not a place to be, though, in bad weather. But the river side is a great place to spend a warm summer afternoon. Strangely, it is a good area to find lost fell walkers, who time and time again take a wrong turn at the cross paths on Esk Hause, Lakeland's highest pass.

Down valley the base rock is pink granite. Iron, which gives it its colour, was mined near Boot and the superb narrow-gauge railway now catering for tourists, especially steam enthusiasts, once carried the ore to the coast and, later, granite from the quarries. The scenic line gives strollers a number of route options. One can go up the wooden ravine of Stanley Ghyll, a place enriched for me by memories of work, and to an airy cliff-top viewpoint, stomach-churning to those who are not expecting it, high above the waterfalls.

But all this is in the south and I have not even touched on the north! What about Borrowdale, with all its access to the fells? Borrowdale of the green and yellow glows of spring! Borrowdale of the fires of autumn! Oh, yes, Borrowdale! Surely my favourite valley. I really cannot say. What about Buttermere's valley, and Ennerdale? The wooded valleys of the south Lakes? And what about the sixteen lakes? Which one is my favourite? What about the solitudes hiding at the Back o' Skiddaw? All the friendly villages?

'You must know the Lake District well,' is often said to me; but I have still a lot to learn: it must take more than a lifetime to cover the whole area. The terrain is so complex; folds within folds, mini valleys branching from the main. Turning off from the path on a fell I have invariably found enclaves to surprise and delight in exploration. I can still find them. A waterfall, perhaps. A small outcrop offering a climbing puzzle. An unexpected view. And although search and rescue has taken me into remote places I can still crest a fell and look out at land on which I have never set foot.

So what about my favourite place? There is no answer. Is it because I find the question rather absurd? Like being asked 'What particular word do you like in a certain piece of poetry?' or 'What particular note in a piece of music?' When the question is put I find it difficult to separate one part from another. The whole is greater than each magnificent part. It has given me a lifetime of pleasure and excitement and will continue to do so, so long, as the bard said, that 'I have eyes to see and heart to enjoy.'